ARCTIC LANDS

ARCTIC LANDS

Baltic
Sea

ope

Black
Sea

Caspian
Sea

ANCIENT
GREECE

Asia

Mediterranean Sea

CHINA

JAPAN

Sea of Japan

ANCIENT EGYPT

MESOPOTAMIA

Persian
Gulf

ANCIENT
INDIA

Red Sea

Arabian
Sea

Bay of
Bengal

South
China
Sea

frica

Indian Ocean

Australia

e of Good Hope

GODS, BELIEFS & CEREMONIES

through the ages

Series Editor Dr. John Haywood

LORENZ BOOKS

First published by Lorenz Books in 2001

© Anness Publishing Limited 2001

Lorenz Books is an imprint of Anness Publishing Limited,
Hermes House, 88–89 Blackfriars Road, London SE1 8HA

www.lorenzbooks.com

This edition distributed in Canada by Raincoast Books, 9050
Shaughnessy Street, Vancouver, British Columbia,
V6P 6M9

Publisher Joanna Lorenz
Managing Editor, Children's Books Gilly Cameron Cooper
Project Editor Rasha Elsaeed
Editorial Reader Jonathan Marshall
Authors Daud Ali, Jen Green, Charlotte Hurdman, Fiona
Macdonald, Lorna Oakes, Philip Steele, Michael Stotter,
Richard Tames
Consultants Nick Allen, Cherry Alexander, Clara Bezanilla,
Felicity Cobbing, Penny Dransart, Jenny Hall, Dr. John
Haywood, Dr Robin Holgate, Michael Johnson, Lloyd Laing,
Jessie Lim, Heidi Potter, Louise Schofield, Leslie Webster,
Designers Simon Borrough, Matthew Cook, John Jamieson,
Joyce Mason, Caroline Reeves, Margaret Sadler, Alison Walker,
Stuart Watkinson at Ideas Into Print, Sarah Williams
Special Photography John Freeman
Stylists Konika Shakar, Thomasina Smith, Melanie Williams

Previously published as part of the *Step Into* series in 14 separate
volumes:
*Ancient Egypt, Ancient Greece, Ancient India, Ancient Japan, Arctic
World, Aztec & Maya Worlds, Celtic World, Chinese Empire, Inca
World, Mesopotamia, North American Indians, Roman Empire,
Viking World, The Stone Age.*

PICTURE CREDITS
b=bottom, t=top, c=centre, l=left, r=right

AKG: 10tl, 13tr, 20tr & 20cl, 42tl, 45bl; B & C Alexander:
54br, 55tl & 55tr; The Ancient Art & Architecture Collection
Ltd: front cover, 5cr, 7tl, 9tr, 12t, 14t & 14b, 15bc & 15tr, 18r,
19tl, 35cr, 38tl, 40bl, 42c, 43c, 44br; Andes Press Agency:
61bl; Bildarchiv Preussischer Kulturbesitz: 11bl & 11t, 12b;
The Bridgeman Art Library: 21tl, 21tr & 21c, 22tr, 26cr, 27tl
& 27c, 34cl, 34tr & 34c, 39r, 46br, 47l, 49bl; The British
Museum: 35cl; Peter Clayton: 8bl, 9tl, 9bl & 9br; Copyright
British Museum: 16l & 16r; Corbis: 52tl & 52b, 53tl, 53c, 53bl
& 53bl, 55c; James Davis: 57br, 58tl; C M Dixon: 4tr, 8br & 8t,
28tl, 36tl, 40tl & 40bl, 41tl, 43tr & 43tl, 46tr, 48l & 48br,
49tr, 50tl, 51tr, 51c & 51bl; E T Archives: 13bl, 28bl, 31tl, 32tl
& 32c, 33bl & 33tr, 46tr, 56tl, 58bl, 59bl; Mary Evans Picture
Library: 18l, 25bl, 29br, 39bl; Werner Forman Archives: title
page, 29tr, 33tl, 44tl, 49cl; Robert Harding: 24b, 25tr; Michael
Holford: 3tr, 5tl, 10bl, 17bl, 35tr, 36cr, 39tl, 41tr & 41bl,
48tr; The Hutchison Library: 23tr, 25tl, 27tr, 30c, 31c; Images
of India: 22b; Link Picture Library: 23br; Manchester Museum:
17tl; Peter Newark: 50br; Michael Nicholson: 37tl, 37cl &
37bl; Roman Baths Museum: 43bl; Scott Polar Research
Institute Ltd: 55l; Mick Sharp: 45tl, 49br, 59tl; South
American Photo Library: 56br, 60tl & 60br, 61tl & 61br;
Statens Historik Museum, Stockholm: 46tr; Tony Stone Images:
23tl; TRIP: 30tr; V & A Picture Library: 23bl, 24t, 57tl &
57tr; ZEFA: 15tl, 17tr, 19tr & 19cr, 29tl & 29b.

10 9 8 7 6 5 4 3 2 1

CONTENTS

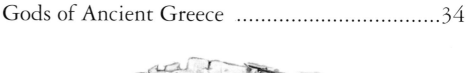

KEY

Look out for the patterns used throughout this book, there is one for each culture

The Stone Age	Japan	North American
Mesopotamia	Ancient Greece	Indians
Ancient Egypt	Roman Empire	The Arctic
India	The Celts	Aztec & Maya
China	The Vikings	Inca Empire

Religion, Ritual, and Myth

Throughout the world, in different centuries, people have expressed their religious beliefs through prayers, ceremonies, offerings, festivals, drama, music, and dancing. We do not know precisely what the ancestors of modern humans thought or felt. However, archaeologists have found evidence of burial rituals dating from more than half a million years ago. Sites discovered in France and the Zagros Mountains in Iran show carefully buried bodies with animal horns and bones around them. If people took the trouble to honor the remains of the dead, they may have believed that a person's spirit lived on, in this world or another one, after their body had decayed. People who hunted for food painted pictures of animals they wanted to find. The paintings may have been for decoration. Some experts believe that they may have been a way in which people tried to contact powerful spirits from the natural world.

Prehistoric venus figurines may have been worshipped as symbols of fertility by early Stone Age people.

It is now believed that cave paintings of animals may have been used in magic ceremonies to guide early hunters or promote fertility.

Rituals and human activities such as art, magic, myth, and ceremonies provide clues to past beliefs. They show us that people gradually developed more complex ways of

Timeline 500,000–2000 B.C.

*c.*500,000 B.C. Early humans living in China perform rituals using the skulls of dead people. This suggests that they either honor the dead person's spirit or fear it.

*c.*75,000 B.C. People in the Middle East start burying some of their dead. They may have believed that a person's spirit lived on, in this world or another one, after their body had decayed.

*c.*30,000 B.C. Cave paintings in Europe show men and women living as hunter-gatherers trying to make contact with powerful spirits from the natural world, to guide and protect them.

*c.*10,000 B.C. People migrate to live in all parts of North and South America. Over the centuries, Native Americans develop many

Animal cave painting

religious beliefs. Some are shared among them all, such as reverence for the natural world, and belief in shamans— magic healers

Shamanic mask worn for special rituals

who can communicate with the spirit world. Others relate to each peoples' own lifestyle and homeland.

500,000 B.C.   30,000 B.C.   10,000 B.C.   9000

explaining the world around them. Many rituals were linked to key stages in peoples' lives, such as birth, death, becoming an adult, or important community events. When people began to farm and live in settled villages, from around 8000 B.C., religion reflected a close relationship with the plants and the seasons. The Aztecs of Mexico, the Celts of Europe, and the Incas of Peru made objects of goddesses who symbolized fertility. Offerings were made to "mother earth" in the hope that in return, divine help would be given to ensure successful crops. Chinese customs encouraged hard work, order, and respect on earth as this created a harmony between heaven, earth, and human beings.

Religions bind societies together. Many settlements grew into market towns, dependent on trade and craftwork and often became centers of religion, too. In Egypt, Greece, and Aztec Mexico, cities were homes to priests and scribes, who guarded religious knowledge and contained splendid temples for worshipping gods. Festivals in India, China, and South America, were opportunities for people to celebrate the gods and natural events, such as the coming of spring or the harvest. As societies grew, people began to ask questions about what religion meant to them personally. What is the meaning of life? Why does

The Inca earth goddess, shown on this gold plate, played an important role in the beliefs of farming peoples, living in the windswept Andes mountains.

During Egyptian ceremonies, priests had to pour sacred water over offerings made to the gods to purify them.

---

*c.*8000 B.C. People begin to live in settled farming villages. New religious beliefs develop, based on the close relationship between farmers, the land, growing plants and the seasons.

*c.*5000 B.C. People begin to live in towns. They build splendid temples for their gods, and to pay for

Stonehenge, a prehistoric stone circle, may have been used for worship

priests to say prayers and make sacrifices (offerings) on the community's behalf.

*c.*3100–30 B.C. The ancient Egyptians worship many gods and goddesses, build magnificent temples, and preserve dead bodies by mummification, so that their spirit will live on after death.

*c.*2300–500 B.C. The civilizations of Akkad, Sumer, Babylon, and Assyria flourish in Mesopotamia (Iraq). Their people worship gods of the sun and moon, and special gods and goddesses who protected their cities and kings.

Sun worshipper

000 B.C.   5000 B.C.   3000 B.C.   2000 B.C.

suffering exist? What happens after death? Does God exist?

Many religions had human versions of their gods on earth. The pharaohs of Egypt and the emperors of China were worshipped as gods. In tribal North America, shamans (healers) had the most important role in the community because they communicated with the spiritual world, thought to control people's daily lives.

In the ancient world, many—rather than one—gods were worshipped. Around 600 B.C., religious leaders appeared in several regions of the world including the Buddha in India and Zoroaster in Persia (Iran). Leaders taught that fulfillment lay beyond this world, in heaven, or in seeking unity with a single God. Philosophers (thinkers), such as Plato in ancient Greece and Confucius in China, began to discuss with their followers the best way to live. Collections of holy scriptures, such as the Hindu Upanishads from India and the Jewish Bible (Torah), were written down to guide believers. This tradition was continued in the 1st century A.D. by the followers of Jesus of Nazareth (Christians) and, in the 7th century A.D. by the prophet Mohammed from Arabia. Mohammed taught Muslims to follow the Koran, a holy text that was believed to be the actual word of God.

People at Holi, the Hindu spring festival, throw colored powders over each other.

Confucious lived at a time of great change in China. He taught people to respect their elders and to work hard.

TIMELINE 1600 B.C.–A.D. 1500

*c.*1600–1122 B.C. The Shang dynasty rules China. People honor the spirits of dead ancestors, and make offerings. They foretell the future by consulting oracle bones.

*c.*1200–600 B.C. The earliest Hindu holy texts, called

Chinese fireworks

Vedas, are written in Sanskrit, the language of the Aryan people who migrate to India at this time.

*c.*800 B.C.–A.D. 100 The Celts are powerful in Europe. They honor nature gods, and make human sacrifices to them. They believe in magic, and are guided by learned priests, called druids.

*c.*604 B.C. Birth of Laozi, religious teacher who founded the Daoist religion in China.

*c.*600–200 B.C. Peak of ancient Greek civilization. The Greeks honor a family of 12 gods, who live on Mount Olympus, and resemble human beings, but possess great powers.

*c.*563–483 B.C. Life of Indian religious leader Siddartha Gautama, known as "Buddha" (the enlightened one). After his death, his teachings spread to many parts of Asia.

*c.*551–479 B.C. Life of Confucius, moral and ethical teacher in China.

1600 B.C.   800 B.C.   600 B.C.   500 B.

This book explores the main religious beliefs from around the world. It starts with the earliest evidence of ceremonies and rituals, and moves through time to see how religions developed in different ways from land to land. The religions of ancient Egypt, Greece and Rome, the Inca, Maya, and Aztec peoples of Central and South America, with their many gods, have disappeared with the civilizations that created them. But some ancient tribal beliefs and ceremonies survive to this day in parts of Africa, the Americas, Australia, and Asia.

You will be able to see how religious beliefs have played in everyday life through the ages. You will be able to compare the ways in which people expressed their faith and depicted their gods

The Celts worshipped their various gods in the form of sculpted images. This clenched-fisted bearded god appears on a large metal bowl.

—in paintings, music and festivals, legends, and traditions that can still be seen today. Most of all, you will have a sense of the rich and varied ways in which people have tried to explain the existence of good and evil, and the reasons for life and death.

The Egyptian pyramids remain a legacy to some of the great beliefs of the past. The Egyptians believed their pharaohs were gods who lived after their bodies had died. They built the pyramids to safeguard their bodies and buried them with their treasures to be used in the afterlife.

c.500 B.C.–A.D. 300 Roman power spreads in Europe. The Romans worship most Greek gods, but give them Roman names, and also family gods of their own.

Shiva, the Hindu god of creation and destruction

A.D. 200 Hinduism is widespread in India. Hindus honor one of two gods, Vishnu or Shiva, as lord of creation.

A.D. 570–632 Life of the Prophet Muhammad, who founded the faith of Islam. This spread from Arabia and is one of the leading world religions.

c.A.D. 700–1100 The Vikings are powerful in Europe. They worship many gods and heroes, and their rich collection of myths and legends explains how the world was created and how it will end.

c.A.D. 960 Christianity starts to spread through the Viking lands.

1469–1539 Life of Guru Nanak, founder of the Sikh religion in India.

1487 Aztecs sacrifice 20,000 captives to consecrate (make holy) the great new temple in their capital city, Tenochtitlan.

Aztec blood sacrifices

D. 200   A.D. 500   1400   1500

Stone Age Beliefs

W E CAN ONLY GUESS at the beliefs of Stone Age people, the earliest ancestors to modern humans. These were the Neanderthal people who lived from 120,000 to 33,000 years ago in Europe and Asia. There is evidence that they were burying their dead, which suggests that they believed in a spirit world. They probably worshipped the spirits of the animals they hunted and other natural things. They made paintings and engravings on rocks and in caves, which may have a magical or religious purpose.

ANCIENT BURIAL
The skull of the skeleton from this burial found in France has been scattered with red ocher earth. Red may have represented blood or life for Stone Age people. Bodies were often buried on their sides, with their knees pulled up to their chins. Tools, ornaments, food, and weapons were put in the graves. Later Stone Age people built elaborate tombs for their dead.

Stone Age people probably thought illnesses and accidents were caused by evil spirits. It may have been the job of a shaman (witch doctor), to speak to the spirits and interpret what should be done.

As farming spread and settlements grew into towns, more organized religions began. Shrines decorated with religious pictures have been found at Çatal Hüyük in Turkey, the site of a well-preserved town dating from around 7000 B.C.

RITUAL ANTLERS
These antlers are from a red stag and were found at Star Carr in England. Some experts think that antlers were worn by a kind of priest called a shaman, perhaps in a coming-of-age ceremony or to bring good luck in that season's hunt.

CLAY GODDESS
This female figure is made from clay and was found at Pazardzik in Bulgaria. Many prehistoric societies worshipped images of the Earth Goddess, or Great Mother. As the mother of the world, she gave life to plants, animals, and humans, and so ensured the future of the human race.

TREPANNING

Cutting a hole in a person's head is called trepanning. It was practiced in prehistoric times from about 5000 B.C. A sharp flint tool was used to cut a hole in the skull in order to let illness escape from the body. Several skulls have been found that show the hole starting to close— evidence that some patients even survived the blood-curdling procedure!

SPELLS AND POTIONS

In many hunter-gatherer societies today, a shaman (witch doctor) can speak with the spirits from the world of the dead. In cultures such as that of the Amazonian Indians, shamans also administer potions from plants to cure illness. They use plants such as quinine, coca, and curare. Stone Age people probably behaved in a similar way. There is evidence that neolithic farmers in northwestern Europe grew poppies and hemp, possibly for use in magic potions and rituals.

poppy

ANCESTOR WORSHIP

Before the people of Jericho in the Near East buried their dead, they removed the skulls. This skull found in Jericho dates from about 6500 B.C. These were covered with plaster and painted to look like the features of the dead person. Cowrie shells were used for eyes. Some experts believe that this was done as a form of ancestor worship.

RITUAL DANCE

A modern painting shows a traditional Australian Aboriginal dance. Traditional ceremonies are an important part of Aboriginal life. Evidence of them has been found on prehistoric sites in Australia. Aboriginal beliefs are designed to maintain the delicate balance between people and their environment.

City Gods of Mesopotamia

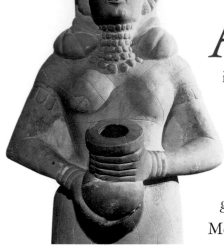

S SETTLEMENTS GREW INTO TOWNS AND CITIES, religious rituals became more complex. Some of the first cities in the world developed in Mesopotamia, most of which is now modern-day Iraq. Each city had its own guardian god and temples were built especially for that god. There were often temples dedicated to members of the god's family, too. The Sumerians, Assyrians, Babylonians, and Akkadian-speaking peoples who lived in Mesopotamia worshipped the same gods and goddesses, but had different names for them. The Sumerians called the Moon-god Nanna, but in Akkadian his name was Sin. The chief Sumerian god was called Enlil, who was often also referred to as King, Supreme Lord, Father, or Creator. According to one Sumerian poem, no one was allowed to look at Enlil, not even the other gods. The Sumerian kings believed that they had been chosen by Enlil.

The god's chief sanctuary was at the city of Nippur. Legends tell that when the Nippur temple was raided by the army of the King of Agade, Enlil was so angry that he caused the Agade dynasty to end.

POWERFUL GODDESS
This statue of a goddess was found in pieces at the palace of Mari on the River Euphrates. Two goddesses like her, pouring water from vases, were part of a scene on the palace courtyard walls. The painting showed a king being invested with royal power by Ishtar, the goddess of love and war.

BEFORE THE GOD
A scene on a 4000-year-old seal shows an official called Lamabazi being led into the presence of a great god by a lesser god. The great god is sitting on the throne, and before him is a brazier for burning incense. Lamabazi is holding his hand in front of his face as a sign of respect for the god.

IN THE BEGINNING
Marduk was the god of Babylon. He is shown here standing on his mushushshu (snake dragon). In the *Epic of Creation*, a Babylonian story about how Marduk created the world, he fought against a female monster, Tiamat, and her son, Kingu. After Marduk had killed them, the other gods made him their king. Marduk then brought the rest of creation into existence. He made models of human beings by mixing some clay with the blood of Kingu and then brought them to life.

CLUES TO IDENTITY

Most of our ideas about what the Mesopotamian gods and goddesses looked like come from their pictures on cylinder seals. This one shows Ishtar, the goddess of love and war, carrying her weapons. She is accompanied by a lion, which was her sacred animal. Shamash, the sun god, is recognizable by the flames coming from him, as he rises between two mountains. Ea, the water god, has streams of water gushing from his shoulders.

FERTILE MIND

Nisaba was originally a goddess of fertility and agriculture, although she later became the goddess of writing. Good harvests were very important to the people of Mesopotamia, and almost everyone ate barley bread and dates. This carving of Nisaba shows her covered with plants. She is wearing an elaborate headdress composed of a horned crown and ears of barley. Flowers sprout from her shoulders, and she is holding a bunch of dates.

GOD OF ASSYRIA

Ashur was the chief god of the Assyrians. It was thought that he was the god who chose the Assyrian kings and went before them into battle. He is often symbolized by the same horned cap as Enlil, the chief Sumerian god. Sometimes he is shown standing on a winged bull or on a mushushshu (snake dragon) like Marduk, the god of Babylon. Both gods were honored in New Year festivals when their priests slapped the reigning king's face, pulled his ears, and made him bow low. The king then said he had served his people properly and was re-crowned for another year.

Bible Links to Mesopotamia

FLOODS
A tale like the Old Testament story of Noah's Ark was found in the library at Nineveh. King Utnapishtim was warned that the god Enlil was going to send a flood and was told to make a boat and take his family, all the animals, and craftsworkers on board. It rained for seven days and seven nights. When it stopped, the king sent out birds to see if the water had gone down. The goddess Ishtar put her necklace in the sky as a sign that this would never happen again.

WHILE THE MESOPOTAMIANS HAD MANY GODS, a faith based on one god developed among the Jews in the area. Many of the people, places, and events in the Jewish holy scriptures (the Old Testament of the Bible) are also told in Mesopotamian history. Several laws and customs relating to marriage and adoption mentioned in the Old Testament are like those of Mesopotamia. Abraham, the father of the Israelite and Arab nations, lived in the Sumerian city of Ur before setting off for the Promised Land. The prophet Jonah was instructed by God to go to the Assyrian city of Nineveh, and the Jewish people were exiled from their Promised Land to Babylon. Assyrian records often include kings and events mentioned in the Old Testament.

One Assyrian king, Shalmaneser III, records his victory at the Battle of Qarqar in Syria. He says he fought against 12 kings, one of whom was Ahab of Israel. This is the first time a king of Israel appears in the history of another country.

DESERT JOURNEY
Abraham, the father of the Jewish and Arab nations, travels from the Sumerian city of Ur to the country God has promised his people. In this painting of the 1800s, Abraham is leading a wandering existence in a desert landscape with his flock of sheep moving from one area to another in search of grazing ground for his animals. However, there would have been no camels at the time he is thought to have lived, about 2000 B.C. They were not used for transport in Mesopotamia until about 1000 B.C.

BLACK OBELISK

The man bowing in front of the Assyrian king, Shalmaneser III, could be Jehu, King of Israel. Israel had been an enemy of Assyria, but Jehu has decided to change sides and become an ally of Assyria. The picture appears on the Black Obelisk, which tells of Shalmaneser III's conquests at war. The writing says that the gifts of the Israelite king are being presented to show his loyalty and win Shalmaneser's approval.

WAR CORRESPONDENTS

The Bible reports that the Assyrian king Sennacherib laid siege to Jerusalem when Hezekiah was king of Judah. It says he withdrew from the siege when an angel attacked his army. In Sennacherib's version of events on this clay prism (a hollow tablet), he does not say he was defeated or that he captured Jerusalem. All he says is that he shut Hezekiah up like a bird in a cage.

EXILE IN BABYLON

The great Babylonian king of the 500s B.C. was Nebuchadnezzar II, who took over many parts of the ancient world that had formerly been part of the Assyrian Empire. In 597 B.C. he attacked Jerusalem, the chief city of the kingdom of Juda, a scene imagined here by a medieval painter. At the end of a successful siege, he took the king, his courtiers, the army, and all the craftworkers to Babylon. There they spent many years far from home, a time known among Jewish people as the Exile. Nebuchadnezzar took treasures from the temple in Jerusalem as booty. He appointed another king, Zedekiah, to rule in Jerusalem. Nebuchadnezzar returned some years later when Zedekiah rebelled and punished him severely.

Pharaoh Gods

HORUS
Horus the falcon god was the son of Isis. He was god of the sky and protector of the reigning pharaoh. The name Horus meant "He who is far above." Here he holds an *ankh*, the symbol of life. The holder of an *ankh* had the power to give life or take it away. Only pharaohs and gods were allowed to carry them.

THE ANCIENT EGYPTIANS believed that the ordered world in which they lived had been created out of chaos. They carried out rituals to prevent chaos and darkness from returning. The pharaohs were honored as god-kings because it was believed the spirit of the gods lived in them. They looked after the everyday world for the gods. More than 2,000 gods were worshipped in ancient Egypt. Many gods were linked to a particular region. The mighty Amun was the god of Thebes. Some gods appeared as animals—Sebek the water god was a crocodile. Gods were also connected with jobs and interests. The hippopotamus goddess, Tawaret, looked after babies and childbirth.

Many ordinary Egyptians understood little about the religion of the court and nobles. They

LOTUS FLOWER
The lotus was a very important flower to the Egyptians. This sacred symbol was used to represent Upper Egypt.

THE GODDESS NUT
Nut, covered in stars, was goddess of the heavens. She is often shown with her body stretched across the sky. The Egyptians believed that Nut swallowed the Sun each evening and gave birth to it the next morning. She was married to the Earth god, Geb, and gave birth to the gods Isis and Osiris.

AMUN OF THEBES

Amun was originally the god of the city of Thebes. He later became popular throughout Egypt as the god of creation. By the time of the New Kingdom, Amun was combined with other powerful gods such as Ra, god of the Sun, and became known as Amun-Ra. He was believed to be the most powerful god of all. Amun is sometimes shown as a ram.

HOLY BEETLES

Scarabs are beetles that were sacred to the ancient Egyptians. Pottery or stone scarabs were used as lucky charms, seals, or as ring decorations. The base of these scarabs was often inscribed with stories telling of some great event.

OSIRIS, KING OF THE UNDERWORLD

The great god Osiris stands dressed as a king. He was one of the most important gods in ancient Egypt, the master of life and the spirit world. He was also the god of farming. Egyptian tales told how Osiris was murdered and cut into pieces by his brother Seth, the god of chaos. Anubis, the jackal-headed god of embalming, gathered the pieces together and his sister, Isis, brought Osiris back to life.

CAT MUMMIES

The Egyptians worshipped gods in the forms of animals from the Old Kingdom onward. The cat goddess Bastet was said to be the daughter of the great Sun god, Ra. Cats were so holy to the Egyptians that at one time many of them were embalmed, wrapped in linen bandages, and preserved as mummies. It is thought that bronze cat figures and these mummified cats were left as offerings to Bastet at her temple.

MIW THE CAT

Cats were holy animals in ancient Egypt. They even had their own god! The Egyptians' love of cats dated back to the early farmers who tamed cats to protect stores of grain from mice. Cats soon became popular pets. The Egyptian word for cat was *miw*, which was like a mew or miaow!

Preparing for the Afterlife

THE EGYPTIANS believed that the dead would need to use their bodies in the next life. They discovered that bodies buried in the desert were often preserved in the dry sand. The bodies dried out and became mummified. Over the ages, the Egyptians became experts at preserving bodies by embalming them.

The methods of mummification varied. The process usually took about 70 days. The brains were hooked out through the nose and the other organs were removed and placed in special jars. Only the heart was left so that it could be weighed in the next life. The body was embalmed by being dried out with salty crystals of natron. Afterward it was stuffed and covered with oils and ointments and then wrapped in bandages. The mummy was then placed inside a series of coffins in the shape of the body.

MUMMY CASE
This beautiful gold case contains the mummy of a priestess. Once the embalmed body had been wrapped in bandages it was placed in a richly decorated coffin. Both the inside and outside would be covered in spells to help the dead person in the underworld. Sometimes more than one coffin was used. The inner coffins would be of brightly painted or gilded wood (*as left*) and the outer coffin would be a stone sarcophagus.

CANOPIC JARS
Special jars were used to store the body's organs. The human-headed jar held the liver. The baboon jar contained the lungs. The stomach was put in the jackal-headed jar and finally the guts were placed in the falcon-headed jar.

CANOPIC JARS

You will need: self-drying clay, rolling pin and board, ruler, modeling tool, sandpaper, masking tape, acrylic paint (white, blue, green, yellow, black), water pot, and brush.

1 Roll out ³/₄ of the clay and cut out a circle about 2³/₄ in. in diameter. This is the base of the jar. Now roll out thin strips of clay. Coil these from the base to make the

2 Carefully press out the bumps between the coils until the sides of the jar are smooth and round. Finally trim the top of the jar with a modeling tool.

3 Now make a lid for the jar. Measure the size needed and cut out a circle of the remaining clay. Shape it into a dome. Model the head of a baboon onto the lid.

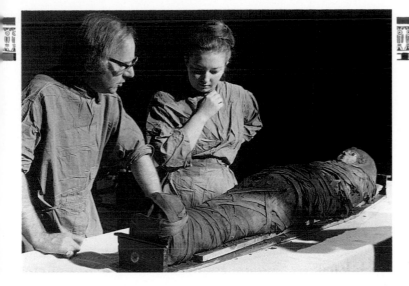

BENEATH THE BANDAGES

Unwrapping a mummy is a delicate operation. Today, archaeologists can use scanning or X-ray equipment to examine the mummies' bodies. It is possible to tell what food they once ate, the work they did, and the illnesses they suffered from. X-rays also show the stuffing used to replace the internal organs.

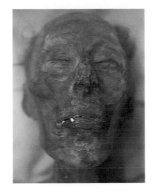

RAMESSES II

This is the unwrapped head of the mummy of Ramesses II. Wadding was placed in his eye sockets to stop the natron (preserving salts) from destroying his features.

THE OPENING OF THE MOUTH CEREMONY

The last ritual before burial was led by a priest wearing the mask of the god Anubis. The human-shaped coffin was held upright and its face was touched with magical instruments. This ceremony enabled the mummy to speak, see, and hear in the next world.

It was believed that any part of a person's body could be used against them. For this reason the organs were removed and stored in canopic jars. Spells written on the jars protected them.

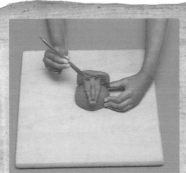

4 Hapy the baboon guarded the mummy's lungs. Use the modeling tool to make the baboon's eyes and long nose. Leave the lid in a warm place to dry.

5 When both the jar and the lid are completely dry, rub them down with sandpaper until they are smooth. The lid should fit snugly on to the jar.

6 It is now time to paint your jar. Use the masking tape to protect the baboon's face and to help you get the stripes straight. Follow the colors in the picture above.

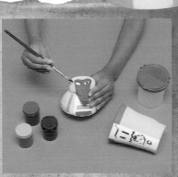

7 Paint hieroglyphs down the front of the jar as shown. Use the design shown above to help you. The canopic jar is now ready for the funeral.

Grand Temples of Egypt

MASSIVE TEMPLES were built in honor of the Egyptian gods. Many can still be seen today. They have great pillars and massive gates, courtyards, and avenues of statues. Once, these would have led to a shrine that was believed to be the home of a god.

Ordinary people did not gather to worship in an Egyptian temple as they might today in a church. Only priests were allowed in the temples. They carried out rituals on behalf of the pharaoh, making offerings of food, burning incense, playing music, and singing. They had complicated rules about washing and shaving their heads, and some had to wear special clothes such as leopard skins. Noblewomen served as priestesses during some ceremonies. Many priests had little knowledge of religion and just served in the temple for three months before returning to their normal work. Other priests studied the stars and spells.

There were many religious festivals during which the god's shrine would be carried to other temples in a great procession. This was when ordinary Egyptians joined in worship. Offerings of food made to the gods were given back to the people for public feasting.

SACRED RITUALS
A priest engaged in a religious ritual wears a leopard skin garment. He is carrying a vase containing sacred water from the temple's holy lake. During ceremonies, this water would have been poured over offering tables to ensure the purity of the gifts made to the gods. Incense would also have been burned to purify the atmosphere of the temple.

KARNAK
This painting by David Roberts shows the massive temple of Karnak as it appeared in 1850. It still stands just outside the modern town of Luxor. The temple's most important god was Amun-Ra. The site also includes courts and buildings sacred to other gods and goddesses, including Mut (a vulture goddess, wife of Amun) and Khons (the Moon god, son of Amun). The Great Temple was enlarged and rebuilt over about 2,000 years.

TEMPLE OF HORUS

A statue of Horus, the falcon god, guards the temple at Edfu. There was a temple on this site during the New Kingdom. However, the building that still stands today dates back to the period of Greek rule. This temple was dedicated to Horus and his wife, the cow goddess Hathor. Inside the temple there are stone carvings showing Horus fighting the enemies of Osiris, his father.

ANUBIS THE EMBALMER

A priest wears the mask of Anubis to embalm a body. This jackal-headed god was said to have prepared the body of the god Osiris for burial. He and his priests had strong links with mummies and the practice of embalming.

KALABSHA TEMPLE

The Kalabsha temple was one of the largest temples in Lower Nubia. In the 1960s, the Aswan Dam was built and Lower Nubia was flooded. Many monuments such as the temples at Abu Simbel and Philae had to be moved. The temple at Kalabsha was dismantled, and its 13,000 blocks of stone were moved to New Kalabsha, where it was rebuilt.

GATEWAY TO ISIS

The temple of Philae (*above*) was built in honor of Isis, the mother goddess. Isis was worshipped all over Egypt and in many other lands, too. Massive gateways called pylons guard the temple of Philae. Pylons guard the way to many Egyptian temples and were used for special ceremonies.

Religions of India

MANY RELIGIONS DEVELOPED IN INDIA. The Aryan people, who settled in northern India from around 1500 B.C., had customs that influenced India's later beliefs. In 500 B.C., a spiritual leader called the Buddha founded Buddhism. This religion was dominant for the next 700 years. In time, the Aryan religion evolved into Hinduism. Many beliefs were the same, but Hinduism discouraged the practice of making animal sacrifices and introduced new gods to replace the Aryan deities. Gradually, Hinduism took over from Buddhism, and has been India's dominant religion ever since.

In the two main types of Hinduism—Vaishnavism and Shaivism—Hindus believe that one god (Vishnu or Shiva) rules the universe. From A.D. 1000, some worshipped the goddess Devi instead. As a result, Hindu mythology seems to have many different gods, but to most Hindus, they are versions of Vishnu, Shiva, or Devi.

TERRIFYING GOD
Shiva appears in the form of a terrifying being wielding a trident. At times, Shiva is associated with the destructive forces of the universe and commands demonic beings, called ganas.

HAPPY GOD
The conch shell and the discus are the symbols of the god Vishnu, who is often shown with blue skin. Vishnu mostly brings happiness, preservation, and kingship. He stands on a lotus flower.

MAKE A GARLAND OF FLOWERS

You will need: Tissue paper in orange, yellow, red, pink, and white, pencil, scissors, white glue, paintbrush, length of string, darning needle.

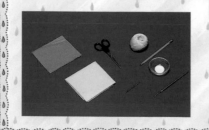

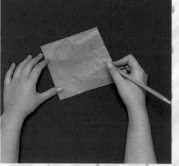

1 Draw simple flower shapes onto sheets of colored tissue paper. If you like, you can lay the sheets of paper in layers, one on top of the other.

2 Using scissors, cut out your flower shapes. Be careful not to tear the tissue paper. Cut the same number of flowers in each color.

3 Scrunch up the tissue flower shapes with your hands. Then uncrumple them, but don't smooth them out too much.

GANESHA

The elephant god, Ganesha, is the son of Shiva. He is god of wisdom and prosperity and is known for his love of sweets. Ganesha is always shown traveling with a rat.

KRISHNA AND RADHA

The god Krishna was an incarnation of Vishnu on earth. Krishna was born as a cowherder. In his youth, he is said to have been adored by many women, but his favorite was Radha. The love of Radha and Krishna is the theme of many Hindu religious songs.

GODDESS OF DEATH AND WAR

Shiva's wife had many forms. The fiercest was Kali, goddess of death. Here, she holds an array of weapons in her many arms. Kings often worshipped Kali before going into battle.

Hindus make garlands of fresh flowers to wear at festivals to honor their gods.

4 Glue the flower shapes together loosely in layers to make larger, single flowers. Use eight layers of tissue paper for each finished flower.

5 Now gently fluff up the layers of tissue paper with your fingers. This will make your flowers look much more impressive.

6 Measure a length of string that is long enough to go around your neck. Start to thread the flowers onto the string to make a garland.

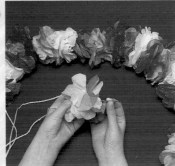

7 Thread all the tissue flowers onto the length of string. When you have secured all the flowers, tie a double knot in the string to finish.

Islam Reaches India

THE MUSLIM RELIGION, called Islam—which means submission to God—was founded in Arabia (present-day Saudi Arabia) by a man named Mohammed in A.D. 622. It spread quickly into the countries around Arabia, and nearly 400 years later, reached India.

In A.D. 1007 Sultan Mahmud, the Muslim leader of the city of Ghazni in Afghanistan, started a series of attacks on northern India to loot the rich temples there. More Islamic leaders followed his example, and by A.D. 1206, Muslim Turks from Central Asia had founded a new kingdom, or Sultanate, based in the city of Delhi. The Delhi Sultanate ruled the region for 300 years.

Islam gradually spread among ordinary Indian people. Islamic sufis (mystics) played an important role in spreading the message of God's love for all people. They worshipped in a very emotional style at their countryside shrines, in a way that the Hindu peasants could understand. By the 1700s, nearly a quarter of India's population was Muslim. They showed great tolerance to other religions and cultures, especially the Hindu faith.

BEAUTIFUL WRITING
This page is from a Persian commentary on the holy book of Muslims, the *Koran*. Muslims were not allowed to represent images, such as humans, animals, or flowers, in art. Instead they developed calligraphy (the art of beautiful writing).

SEAFARING SETTLERS
The Indian Ocean was controlled by Muslim traders from about A.D. 700. They arrived along the southwestern coast of India on their way to Indonesia and China, and were among the earliest Muslims to settle in India. These traders followed Muslim law. Different Muslim laws spread in India through further Muslim invasions from Turkey and Afghanistan in the 1100s and 1200s.

FROM TEMPLE TO MOSQUE

The Quwat al-Islam, a large mosque in Delhi, was built out of parts of destroyed temples of older faiths. It has two architectural features that were introduced to India by Islam. One feature is the arch, the other is the use of mortar for sticking bricks together. The mosque was built by the Delhi Sultanate in 1193.

HOLY MEN

Sufis (mystics) gather together to pray. Sufism was a type of Islam that preached that people's souls can communicate to God through ecstatic music, singing and dancing. Sufism came into prominence in Persia in the A.D. 900s. By about 1100 it had also gained a foothold in the northwest of

FAMILY TOMB

A man cycles toward a tomb of one of the later Sultans of Delhi. The tomb is in the gardens of the Lodi family, the last rulers of the Delhi Sultanate. The last Lodi Sultan was defeated in battle by the Mughal prince Babur, in 1526.

SUFI SHRINE

This tomb-shrine, or dargah, in Rajgir, honors a famous sufi saint. Sufi teachers were called pirs, or shaikhs. They often had a large number of followers.

Sikhs of India

AS ISLAM SPREAD through northern India, Hinduism, and Islam existed side by side. In the Punjab region of northern India, a new religion emerged that had elements of both. It was called Sikhism, and was founded by a man called Guru (teacher) Nanak (1469–1539). Sikhism rejected the strict Hindu caste system and adopted the Islamic idea that all people are equal before God, but kept many aspects of Hindu ritual. Sikhs worshipped in temples called gurdwaras (abode of the gurus). After Nanak, there were nine more gurus. The fifth, Arjan, founded the Golden Temple at Amritsar, which later became the holiest of all gurdwaras. He also wrote the Sikh holy book, or *Adi Granth*.

In the 1600s, the Muslim Mughal rulers in Delhi became concerned about the growth of this new religion. They began to persecute the Sikhs and killed Arjan and another guru. The tenth guru, Gobind Singh, decided that Sikhs should protect themselves and founded a military order called the khalsa. Members carried a comb and dagger, wore a steel bangle, short pants, and did not cut their hair. Sikh men took the title Singh (lion). After the death of Gobind Singh in 1708, there were no more gurus, but Sikhs continued to live by the teachings of the *Adi Granth*.

LETHAL TURBAN
A Sikh war turban is decorated with weapons that could be removed and used against the enemy during battle. Metal throwing rings could slice heads off, while "claws" were for disemboweling people.

THE GOLDEN TEMPLE
The greatest Sikh temple is the Golden Temple in the Sikh holy city of Amritsar. The temple was built by Guru Arjan Singh (1581–1606). Its white marble walls and domes are decorated with gold. The city of Amritsar is named after the lake that surrounds the temple. Sikhs worship in their temples in large congregations (groups). Free kitchens are attached to Sikh temples, where all can eat.

SYMBOLIC COMB
This close-up picture of a Sikh turban shows the kangha, a comb that is pinned to the center. The kangha is one of the five signs of the Sikh religion. Sikh men do not cut their hair—another sign of Sikhism.

THE SACRED BOOK
The *Adi Granth* is the sacred book of the Sikhs. Its text was compiled by Guru Arjan Singh in the late 1500s. After the death of the last teacher, Guru Gobind Singh, Sikhs came to accept these scriptures as the symbol of God. They took over the role of the teacher from the Gurus.

A MILITARY MAHARAJA
The Maharaja Ranjit Singh (1799–1838) holds court. The water tank of the Golden Temple can be seen in the background. Ranjit Singh led the Sikh army to victory against Afghan warlords and the collapsing Mughal Empire. He established a separate Sikh kingdom in the Punjab region of India.

AN ABLE WARRIOR
A Sikh soldier sits on a cushion in this portrait from the 1800s. When the British ruled India, they recruited many Sikhs into their army. Sikhs were regarded as one of India's most warlike peoples.

Festivals and Ceremonies in India

RITUAL CEREMONIES in India go back to Aryan times (1500 B.C.), when there were fire sacrifices throughout the year. After the growth of Buddhism, priests developed a set of rites for important events such as marriages, caste initiations, and funerals, which Hindus then used for centuries. Many temple festivals developed, too. Some, such as Navaratri and Dasara, honored fierce goddesses. Diwali was a festival of lights in honor of the goddess Lakshmi. In spring, people played games at the fertility festival of Holi.

HANDY HENNA
Using henna to mark the hands and feet was a common practice in India, and is still part of marriage ceremonies. Henna is a plant extract that is mixed into a paste with water and used to make patterns on the skin. The paste dyes the skin red.

Generally, Muslims had fewer and less elaborate rituals. Islamic festivals included Eid al-Fitr after Ramadan, the month of fasting, and Eid al-Adha to commemorate Abraham's attempted sacrifice of his son, Isaac. Muslims also adopted some of the customs and practices of the Hindus.

A FESTIVAL OF FUN
The Vasantotsava (or modern Holi) was a festival of play and courtship that took place in the spring. Men and women threw colored powders and squirted colored waters over one another with syringes as they ran around the streets and gardens of the city.

TABLA DRUM
You will need: 22 x 17 in. sheet of thick cardboard, measuring tape, scissors, compasses, pencil, sticky tape, strips of newspaper, flour and water or wallpaper paste, bowl, fine sandpaper, calico fabric, awl, red-brown and blue paint, paintbrushes, darning needle, twine, white glue.

1 Cut out a cardboard rectangle 21½ x 8¼ in. Cut slits along both long edges. Use the compasses to measure a card circle with a diameter of 6¼ in.

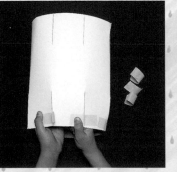

2 Roll the rectangle to form a cylinder with a diameter of 6¼ in. and tape. Tape the slits so that the drum tapers at each end. Tape the circle to one end.

3 Cover the cylinder with 3 layers of newspaper strips soaked in paste or flour and water. Let it dry between layers. Smooth the edges with sandpaper.

CEREMONY AROUND THE FIRE

A bride, with her face covered, is led into the marriage pandal (ceremonial awning), which is covered with mango and lime leaves to bring good luck. The bride will follow her husband around the fire. Hindu marriages still take place in the home around a sacrificial fire, and are administered by a Brahmin priest.

END OF FASTING

Muslim men take part in Eid festivities, in Bombay. Muslim men pray in public congregations at a mosque and give zakat (gifts) to the poor. Then they celebrate with friends and families.

PILGRIMAGE TO MECCA

Muslim pilgrims travel by camel to the city of Mecca, in Arabia (modern Saudi Arabia). Muslims must travel to Mecca once in their lifetime, if possible. The journey is called the haj.

DEATH OF AN IMAM

A passion play with music and drumming is enacted in the streets to celebrate Muharram, the first month of the Muslim calender. For Shia Muslims, the tenth day of Muharram is one of dramatic public mourning to commemorate the death of an imam (spiritual leader) named Husain.

The tabla drum was played at ceremonies and festivals.

4 Cut a circle of calico with a diameter of 10 in. Prick holes around the edge with an awl. Paint the tabla with two coats of red-brown paint.

5 Thread the needle with a long piece of twine and knot. Place the calico over the tabla's open end. Push the needle and thread through a hole in the calico.

6 Pass the twine across the base and through a hole on the other side of the fabric. Pull the twine tight, to stretch the fabric. Repeat all the way around the tabla.

7 Paint a pattern on to the calico. Then apply a coat of watered down white glue. This will help to shrink the calico and pull it tight over the tabla.

Chinese Religions

"THREE TEACHINGS FLOW INTO ONE" is an old saying in China. The three teachings are Daoism, Confucianism, and Buddhism. In China they gradually merged together over the ages.

The first Chinese peoples believed in various gods and goddesses of nature, in spirits, and demons. The spirit of nature and the flow of life inspired the writings that are said to be the work of Laozi (born *c.*604 B.C.). His ideas formed the basis of the Daoist religion. The teachings of Kong Fuzi (Confucius) come from the same period of history but they stress the importance of social order and respect for ancestors as a source of happiness. At this time another great religious teacher, the Buddha, was preaching in India. Within 500 years, Buddhist teachings had reached China and by the Tang dynasty (A.D. 618–906), Buddhism was the most popular religion. Islam arrived at this time and won followers in the northwest. Christianity also came into China from Persia, but few Chinese were converted to this religion until the 1900s.

THE MERCIFUL GODDESS
Guanyin was the goddess of mercy and the bringer of children. She was a holy figure for all Chinese Buddhists.

DAOISM—A RELIGION OF HARMONY
A young boy is taught the Daoist belief in the harmony of nature. Daoists believe that the natural world is in a state of balance between two forces—yin and yang. Yin is dark, cool, and feminine, while yang is light, hot and masculine. The two forces are combined in the black and white symbol on the scroll.

PEACE THROUGH SOCIAL ORDER
Kong Fuzi (Confucius) looks out on to an ordered world. He taught that the well-being of society depends on duty and respect. Children should obey their parents and wives should obey their husbands. The people should obey their rulers, and rulers should respect the gods. All of the emperors followed the teachings of Confucianism.

FREEDOM FROM DESIRE

Chinese monks carved huge statues of the Buddha from rock. Some can be seen at the Mogao caves near Dunhuang, where temples were built as early as A.D. 366. The Buddha taught that suffering is caused by our love of material things. Buddhists believe that we are born over and over again until we learn to conquer this desire.

ISLAM IN CHINA

This is part of the Great Mosque in Xian (ancient Chang'an), built in the Chinese style. The mosque was founded in A.D. 742, but most of the buildings in use today date from the Ming dynasty (1368–1644). Islam first took root in China in about A.D. 700. Moslem traders from Central Asia brought with them the Koran, the holy book of Islam. It teaches that there is only one god, Allah, and that Mohammed is his prophet.

TEMPLE GUARDIANS

Gilded statues of Buddhist saints ward off evil spirits at Puningsi, the Temple of Universal Peace, near Chengde. The temple was built in 1755 in the Tibetan style. It is famed for its Mahayana Hall, a tower roofed in gilded bronze.

Celebrations in China

THE CHINESE FESTIVAL best known around the world today is the New Year or Spring Festival. Its date varies according to the traditional Chinese calendar, which is based on the phases of the moon. The festival is marked by dancers carrying a long dragon through the streets, accompanied by loud, crackling firecrackers to scare away evil spirits. The festival has been celebrated for more than 2,000 years and has always been a time for family feasts and village carnivals. The doorways of buildings are traditionally decorated with handwritten poetry on strips of red paper to bring luck and good fortune for the coming year.

Soon after New Year, sweet dumplings made of rice flour are prepared for the Lantern Festival. Paper lanterns are hung out to mirror the first full moon of the year. This festival began during the Tang dynasty (A.D. 618–906). In the eighth month of the year, the autumn full moon is marked by the eating of special moon cakes.

Chinese festivals are linked to agricultural seasons. They include celebrations of sowing and harvest, dances, horse races, and the eating of specially prepared foods.

DANCING ANIMALS
Chinese New Year parades are often headed by a lion (*shown above*) or dragon. These are carried by dancers accompanied by crashing cymbals. The first month of the Chinese calendar begins on the first full moon between January 21 and February 19.

HORSE RACING
The Mongols, who invaded China in the 1200s, brought with them their love of horses and superb riding skills. Today, children as young as three years old take part in horse-racing festivals in northern China and Mongolia. Archery and wrestling competitions are also regularly held.

MAKE A LANTERN

You will need: thick cardboard, pencil, ruler, scissors, compasses, glue and brush, red tissue paper, blue paint, paintbrush, water pot, thin blue and yellow cardboard, wire, tape, bamboo stick, torch, fringing fabric.

Frame (x4) — 10 in. × 7 in.
½ in.
Side (x4) — 1 in. × 6½ in.
End (x2) — 7 in. × 7 in.

Using the measurements above, draw the 10 pieces on to thick card (pieces not drawn to scale). Cut out pieces with scissors.

1 Using compasses, draw an 3¼ in. diameter circle in the middle of one of the end pieces. Cut out the circle with scissors. Glue on the 4 sides, as shown.

2 Glue together the frame pieces. Then glue the end pieces on to the frame. When dry, cover frame with red tissue paper. Glue one side at a time.

DRAGON BOATS

In the fifth month of the Chinese year, races are held in the Dragon Boat festival. This is in memory of a famous statesman called Qu Yuan, who drowned himself in 278 B.C. when his advice to his ruler was ignored. Rice dumplings are eaten at the Dragon Boat festival every year in his memory.

CHINESE LANTERNS

Elaborate paper lanterns brighten up a wedding in the 1800s during the Qing dynasty. Lanterns were also strung up or paraded on poles at other private celebrations and during Chinese festivals.

Light up your lantern by placing a small torch inside it. Decorate with a fringe. Now you can join in Chinese celebrations!

3 Paint top of lantern blue. Cut borders out of blue card. Glue to top and bottom of frame. Stick a thin strip of yellow card to bottom border.

4 Make 2 small holes opposite each other at top of lantern. Pass the ends of a loop of wire through each hole. Bend and tape ends to secure wire.

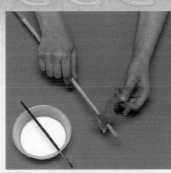

5 Make a hook from thick cardboard. Split end opposite hook. Glue and wrap around bamboo stick. Hang lantern by wire loop from hook.

Ancient Japanese Faith

ALMOST ALL Japanese people in history followed a very ancient religious faith called Shinto. Shinto means the way of the gods. It developed from a central idea that all natural things had a spiritual side. These natural spirits—called *kami* in Japanese—were often kindly, but could be powerful or even dangerous. They needed to be respected and worshipped. Shinto also encouraged the worship of ancestors, spirits who could guide, help, and warn. Special priests, called shamans, made contact with the spirits by chanting, fasting, or by falling into a trance.

Shinto spirits were honored at shrines that were often built close to sites of beauty or power, such as waterfalls or volcanoes. Priests guarded the purity of each shrine, and held rituals to make offerings to the spirits. Each Shinto shrine was entered through a *torii* (large gateway), which marked the start of the sacred space. *Torii* always had the same design—they were based on the ancient perches of birds waiting to be sacrificed.

AT THE SHRINE
A priest worships by striking a drum at the Grand Shrine at Izu, one of the oldest Shinto shrines in Japan. A festival is held there every August, with processions, offerings, and prayers. An *omikoshi* (portable shrine) is carried through the streets, so that the spirits can bring blessings to everyone.

OFFERINGS TO THE SPIRITS
Worshippers at Shinto shrines leave offerings for the *kami* (spirits) that live there. These offerings are neatly wrapped barrels of *sake* (rice wine). Today, worshippers also leave little wooden plaques with prayers on them.

VOTIVE DOLLS
You will need: self-drying clay, 2 balsa wood sticks (4¾ in. long), ruler, paints, paintbrush, water pot, modeling clay, silver foil, red paper, gold paper, scissors, pencil, glue stick, optional basket and dowelling stick.

1 Place a ball of clay on the end of each of the balsa sticks. On one of the sticks, push the clay down so that it is ¼ in. from the end. This will be the man.

2 Paint hair and features on the man. Stand it up in modeling clay to dry. Repeat with the woman. Cover the ¼ in. excess stick on the man's head in foil.

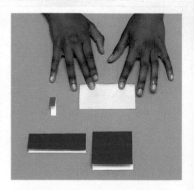

3 Take two pieces of red paper, 2½ x 5½ in. and 2½ x 4 in. Fold them in half. Take two pieces of gold paper, 4¼ x 4 in. and ½ x 2¾ in. Fold in half.

LUCKY GOD

Daikoku is one of seven lucky gods from India, China, and Japan that are associated with good fortune. In Japan, he is the special god of farmers, wealth, and of the kitchen. Daikoku is recognized by both Shinto and Buddhist

HOLY VOLCANO

Fuji-San (Mount Fuji) has been honored as a holy place since the first people arrived in Japan. Until 1867, women were not allowed to set foot on Fuji's holy ground.

FLOATING GATE

This *torii* at Miyajima (Island of Shrines), in southern Japan, is built on the seashore. It appears to float on the water as the tide flows in. Miyajima was sacred to the three daughters of the Sun.

In some regions of Japan, dolls like these are put on display in baskets every year at Hinamatsuri (Girls' Day), on March 3.

4 Take the folded red paper (2½ x 5½ in.) This is the man's *kimono*. Cut a triangular shape out of the bottom. Cut a neck hole out at the folded end.

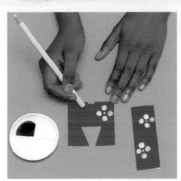

5 Dip the blunt end of the pencil in white paint. Fleck a pattern onto the red paper. Add the central dots using the pencil tip dipped in paint.

6 Slip the man's head and body into the red paper *kimono*. Then take the larger piece of gold paper and fold around the stick, as shown. Glue in place.

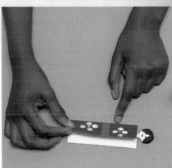

7 Now stick the gold paper (⅓ x 2¾ in.) onto the woman's *kimono*, in the middle. Slip the woman's head and body into the *kimono*. Glue in place.

Gods of Ancient Greece

THE GODS OF THE ANCIENT GREEKS had many human characteristics. They looked like ordinary people and felt emotions that led them to quarrel and fall in love. However, the gods also had magical powers and were immortal (they could live forever). With these powers, the gods could become invisible, or disguise themselves, or turn people into animals. The gods were thought to influence all parts of human life. They were kept busy with requests for help, from curing illness to ensuring a victory in war. In order to keep on the right side of the gods, the Greek people made sacrifices, left offerings, and said prayers. Communities financed the building of temples, such as the Parthenon in Athens. They paid for priests to look after the buildings and to organize festivals in honor of the gods.

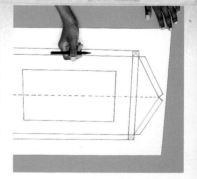

WILD GODDESS
Artemis was the goddess of wild places and animals, hunting, and the moon. She was a skilful archer, whose arrows caused death and plagues. The power to heal was another of her attributes.

WINGED MESSENGER
Hermes was the god of eloquence and good luck. He was known for his mischievous and adventure-seeking nature. Zeus made him a messenger to the gods to try and keep him occupied and out of trouble.

KING OF THE GODS
Zeus ruled over earth and heaven from Mount Olympus, (a real place on the border of Macedonia). He was thought to be a fair god who upheld order and justice. Wrongdoers could be punished with thunderbolts thrown by him.

PARTHENON
You will need: two pieces of white cardboard 24½ x 15¼ in., ruler, black felt-tip pen, shoebox, scissors, blue, red, and cream paint, paintbrush, white glue, piece of red corrugated cardboard (approximately 15¼ x 11¼ in.), masking tape, craft knife, 63 in. of balsa wood.

1 Draw a horizontal line across the center of the cardboard. Place the shoebox in the middle. Draw around it. Draw a second box 2¾ in. away from this.

2 Draw a third box ¾ in. away from the second. Extend the lines of the second box to meet the third, to form four tabs, one in each corner.

3 To make the ends of the roof, draw half a diamond shape along the edge of the second box. Add on two rectangular tabs ½ in. deep.

SYMBOLS

Each god and goddess was thought to be responsible for particular aspects of daily life. Each was represented by a symbol. Wheat symbolized Demeter, goddess of living things. Dionysus, god of the vine and wine, was appropriately represented by grapes.

wheat   grapes

GRAPES OF JOY

The god Dionysus was admired for his sense of fun. As god of fertility, the vine, and wine, he was popular with both male and female worshippers. However, his followers were too enthusiastic for some city-states, which banned celebrations in his name.

LOVE AND PROTECTION

Aphrodite was the goddess of love and beauty. Her vanity was instrumental in causing one of the biggest campaigns in Greek folklore, the Trojan War. Aphrodite promised to win Paris (son of the king of Troy) the love of the most beautiful mortal woman in the world—Helen. In return, Paris was to name Aphrodite as the most beautiful of all the goddesses. However, Helen was already married to the king of Sparta. When she left him to join Paris, the Greeks declared war on Troy. A bloodthirsty war followed in which heroes and gods clashed.

A POWERFUL FAMILY

Hera was the wife of Zeus and goddess of marriage. She was revered by women as the protector of their married lives. Her own marriage was marked by conflicts between herself and her husband. Her jealousy of rivals for her unfaithful husband's affections led her to persecute them. She was also jealous of Heracles, who was Zeus' son by another woman. Hera sent snakes to kill Heracles when he was a baby. Fortunately for Heracles, he had inherited his father's strength and killed the snakes before they harmed him.

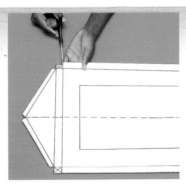

4 Repeat step 3 for the other end of the roof. Cut out both ends of the roof and cut into the four corner tabs. Get your painting equipment ready.

5 Turn the roof piece over. Draw and then paint the above design on to each end piece. Paint a blue, ½ in. margin along each side. Let dry.

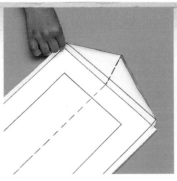

6 Turn the cardboard over. Fold up all the sides of the second box. Fold in each corner tab and glue to its adjoining side. Fold down the rectangular tabs.

7 Cut the piece of red corrugated cardboard in half. Stick them together with tape, along the unridged side. Turn over and fold along the middle.

Temples and Festivals in Greece

FESTIVALS TO HONOR THE GODS were important public occasions in ancient Greece. At the heart of each festival was a temple. At festival time, people flocked to the cities from the countryside. The greatest festivals were occasions of splendor and celebration. They involved processions, music, sports, prayers, animal sacrifices, and offerings of food, all of which took place at the temple. The earliest Greek temples were built of wood, and none have survived. Later, temples built from stone echoed the simplicity of tree trunks in their columns and beams. The finest temples were made from marble. They were often decorated with brightly painted friezes, showing mythical stories of gods, goddesses, and heroes. No expense was spared because temples were thought to be the gods' earthly homes. Each temple housed a statue of the god to which it was dedicated. The statues were usually elaborate and occasionally made from precious materials such as gold and ivory.

A Woman's Role
This vase in the shape of a woman's head was made about 600 B.C., probably for a temple dedicated to Apollo, the handsome god of music. Religion was one of the few areas of life outside the home in which women were allowed to take an active part. They served as priestesses in some cults and were often thought to have the gift of seeing into the future.

Grand Entrance
The monumental gateway to the temple complex at the Acropolis in Athens was called the Propylaea. The temple beside it honored the city's guardian goddess, Athena.

8 Glue the ends of the corrugated cardboard to the folded up edges of the painted cardboard. Let dry. This piece forms the roof to your temple.

9 Draw around the shoebox, onto the second piece of cardboard. Draw another box 2¾ in. away. Cut it out, leaving a ½ in. border. This is the temple base.

10 Ask an adult to help you with this step. Cut out 32 columns from balsa wood. Each must be 2 in. in height. Paint them cream and let dry.

11 Mark eight points along each edge of the second box by drawing around a column piece. Draw them an equal distance from each other.

A BIRTHDAY PARADE

A parade of horsemen, chariots, and people leading sacrificial animals all formed part of the procession of the Panathenaic festival. This was held once a year, in Athens, to celebrate the goddess Athena's birthday. Every fourth year, the occasion involved an even more elaborate ceremony which lasted for six days. During the festivities, the statue of Athena was presented with a new robe.

A TEMPLE FOR THREE GODS

The Erectheum was built on the Acropolis, looking down on Athens 328 ft. below. Unusually for a Greek temple, it housed the worship of more than one god: the legendary king Erectheus; Athena, guardian goddess of the city of Athens, and Poseidon, god of the sea. The columns in the shape of women are called caryatids.

BUILDING MATERIALS

Big buildings, such as temples, were often put up near a quarry or navigable water. Limestone was the most commonly used stone, and pine and cypress the commonest woods. Costly marble and cedar were reserved for temples and palaces.

marble

limestone

pine

THE LION'S MOUTH

This gaping lion is actually a waterspout from an Athenian temple built in about 570 B.C. Although rainfall in Greece is low, waterspouts were necessary to allow storm water to drain off buildings with flat roofs. The lion was chosen as a symbol of strength and power.

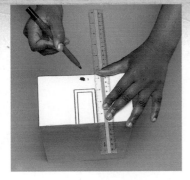

12 Draw a door onto a short end of the shoebox. Glue the roof onto the top of the shoebox. Paint the ½ in. border on the temple base, blue.

13 Glue the columns into place, between the roof and the base. Dab glue onto their ends. Position them on the circles marked out in step 11.

The magnificent Parthenon temple housed a 50 ft.-high statue of Athena that was made of gold and ivory.

The Ancient Greek Underworld

PEOPLE IN ANCIENT GREECE lived only about half as long as people in the West do today. It was common for sickly children to die in infancy. Large numbers of men were killed in battle, women often died in childbirth, and epidemics could wipe out whole communities.

Most Greeks believed that after death, their souls roamed the Underworld, a cold and gloomy region where the wicked were sent to be punished. Achilles, the hero in the Greek epic poem, *The Odyssey,* says, "I'd rather be a common laborer on earth working for a poor man than lord of all the legions of the dead." Few people were thought good enough to be sent to the Isles of the Blessed. If they were, they could spend eternity amusing themselves with sports and music. People who had led exceptional lives (such as the hero Heracles) were destined to become gods and live on Mount Olympus, the home of the gods.

When someone died, their body was either buried or cremated. The Greeks believed that only when the body or ashes had been covered with earth, could its spirit leave for the Underworld. Graves contained possessions for use in the afterlife, and women left offerings of food and drink at the graveside to help the spirits.

FRAGRANT FAREWELL
Graves were sometimes marked with lekythoi, white clay flasks holding a perfumed oil that had been used to anoint the body. The lekythoi were usually painted with farewell scenes, funerals, or images of the dead.

FOOD FOR THOUGHT
The tradition of leaving food at gravesides began in Mycenaean times. Then people could be buried with their armor, cooking pots and even pets and slaves to accompany them. By 300 B.C. the Greeks were leaving food such as wine and eggs at gravesides as nourishment for the dead.

wine

eggs

A DIVE INTO THE UNKNOWN
The figure on the painting above is shown leaping from life into the ocean of death. The pillars were put up by Heracles to mark the end of the known, living world. This diver was found painted on the walls of a tomb.

TUG OF LOVE

This painting from a vase shows Persephone with her husband, Hades, ruler of the underworld. Hades dragged Persephone from earth down to the Underworld. Her distraught mother, the goddess Demeter, neglected the crops to search for her. Zeus intervened and decided that Persephone would spend six months of every year with her mother and the other six with Hades. Whenever her daughter returned in spring, Demeter would look after the crops. However, Demeter grew sad each time her daughter went back to the Underworld and wintertime would set in.

LAST JOURNEY

The body of a dead person was taken from the home to the grave by mourners bearing tributes. To express their grief, they might cut off their hair, tear at their cheeks with their nails until blood flowed, and wear black robes. If there was a funeral feast at the graveside, the dishes were smashed afterwards and left there.

ROYAL TOMB

Women were less likely to be honored by tombstone portraits than men. Philis, seen above, was an exception to this rule, possibly because she was the daughter of a powerful Spartan king. Athens enforced a law against extravagant tombs. No more than ten men could be employed for any more than three days to build one.

Roman Gods

WHEN THE ROMANS conquered Greece in 146 B.C., they adopted many of the ancient Greek gods. Some gods were renamed in Latin, the language of the Roman Empire. Jupiter (Zeus in Greek), the sky god, was the most powerful god. Venus (Aphrodite) was the goddess of love, Mars (Ares) was the god of war, Ceres (Demeter) goddess of the harvest, and Mercury god of merchants. Household gods protected the home. Splendid temples were built in honor of the gods, and special festivals were held during the year, with processions, music, offerings, and animal sacrifices. The festivals were often public holidays. The mid-winter festival of Saturnalia, in honour of Saturn, lasted up to seven days. As the Roman Empire grew, many Romans adopted the religions of other peoples, such as the Egyptians and the Persians.

CHIEF GOD
Jupiter was the chief god of the Romans. He was the all-powerful god of the sky. The Romans believed he showed his anger by hurling a thunderbolt to the ground.

ONE TO ALL
The Pantheon in Rome was a temple to all the gods. It was built between A.D. 118 and 128. Its mosaic floor, interior columns, and high dome still remain exactly as they were built.

DIANA THE HUNTRESS
Diana was the goddess of hunting and the Moon. In this detail from a floor mosaic, she is shown poised with a bow and arrow, ready for the hunt. Roman gods were often the same as the Greek ones, but were given different names. Diana's Greek name was Artemis.

A TEMPLE TO THE GODS

You will need: thick stiff cardboard, thin cardboard, old newspaper, scissors, balloon, white glue, ruler, pencils, masking tape, drinking straws, acrylic paints, paintbrush, water pot, modeling clay.

dome base — 7 in.

roof — 16¼ in.

roof — 1¼ in. / 2¾ in. / 2¾ in. / ½ in. / ½ in. / 4¾ in.

roof

base — 7 in.

portico — 2 in. / 2 in. / 4¾ in. / 8¾ in.

roof — 1¼ in. / 6¼ in.

3½ in. / 4¾ in. / 2¾ in. / 5½ in.

Cut out pieces of card following the measurements shown.

1 Blow up the balloon. Cover it in strips of newspaper pasted on with glue. Keep pasting until you have a thick layer. Let dry. Then burst the balloon and cut out a dome.

PRIESTS OF ISIS

The Egyptian mother-goddess Isis had many followers throughout the Roman Empire. This painting shows priests and worshippers of Isis taking part in a water purification ceremony. The ceremony would have been performed every afternoon.

BLESS THIS HOUSE

This is a bronze statue of a *lar* or household god. Originally gods of the countryside, the *lares* were believed to look after the family and the home. Every Roman home had a shrine to the *lares*. The family, including the children, would make daily offerings to the gods.

MITHRAS THE BULL-SLAYER

Mithras was the Persian god of light. He is shown here, in a marble relief from a temple, slaying a bull. This bull's blood was believed to have brought life to the Earth. The cult of Mithras spread through the whole Empire, and was particularly popular with Roman soldiers. However, only men were allowed to worship Mithras.

The Pantheon was built of brick and then clad in stone and marble. Its huge dome, with a diameter of more than 141 ft., was the largest ever constructed until the 1900s.

2 Put the dome on its cardboard base and draw its outline. Cut out the center of the base to make a halo shape. Make a hole in the top of the dome. Bind the pieces together.

3 Glue together the base pieces. Cut a piece of thin cardboard to go around the base circle. This will be the circular wall. Use masking tape to holdd the portico in shape.

4 Cut some straws into eight pieces, each 2½ in. long. These will be the columns for the entrance colonnade. Glue together the roof for the entrance. Secure with tape.

5 Glue together the larger pieces, as shown. Position each straw column with a small piece of modeling clay at its base. Glue on the entrance roof. Paint your model.

Protectors of Celtic Tribes

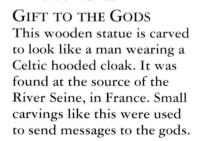

HERE ARE MANY surviving traces of Celtic religion, in descriptions by Roman writers, in carvings and statues, in place names, in collections of religious offerings, and in myths and legends. Yet there are many things we do not know or fully understand about Celtic beliefs. This is because the Celts believed that holy knowledge was too important to be written down. It seems almost certain, however, that they worshipped gods who protected the tribe and gave strength in war, and goddesses who protected homes and brought fertility. Some gods were associated with the sky, and some goddesses with the earth. Gods and spirits controlled the elements and natural forces, such as water and thunder. They were given different names in different parts of the Celtic world, which covered large areas of central and northwestern Europe. Gods and goddesses were worshipped close to water and in groves of trees. The Celts believed that dreadful things would happen if they did not make sacrifices of their most valuable possessions, including living things, to the gods.

GIFT TO THE GODS
This wooden statue is carved to look like a man wearing a Celtic hooded cloak. It was found at the source of the River Seine, in France. Small carvings like this were used to send messages to the gods.

HANDS HELD HIGH
From the Gundestrup bowl, this bearded god holds his hands up. Such a gesture may have been used by druids (Celtic priests) when praying. The clenched fists are a sign of power.

MAKE THE GUNDESTRUP BOWL

You will need: plastic bowl, silver foil, scissors, cardboard strip 4¾ x 33 in., felt-tip pen, modeling clay, white glue, double-sided tape, awl, paper fasteners.

1 Find a plastic bowl that measures about 10¼ in. in diameter across the top. Cover the bowl on the inside and outside with silver foil.

2 Use the pair of scissors to trim any excess foil, as shown. Ensure that you leave enough foil to turn over the top edge neatly.

3 Divide the cardboard into six sections. Leave 1¼ in. at the end. Draw a god figure in each section. Make a clay version of the figure. Glue it on top.

BURIED IN A BOG

The remains of this Celtic man were found in a peat bog in northern England. He died some time between A.D.1 and A.D.200. He was sacrificed by being killed in three different ways: having been strangled, had his throat cut, and struck on the head. Like the three-mothers carving, this shows the Celts' use of the number three for religious purposes.

HORSES AND WAR

According to Roman writers, Epona was the Celtic goddess of war. Epona was worshipped by many Roman soldiers who spent time on duty in Celtic lands. This Roman-style carving shows Epona with a horse. It was found in northern France.

HUMAN SACRIFICE

Celtic priests, called druids, sometimes sacrificed human beings and animals as offerings to the gods. This scene from the Gundestrup bowl shows a giant-sized figure, maybe a god, holding a human sacrifice.

The famous Gundestrup bowl, which inspired your model, was made in eastern Europe some time between 200 B.C. and 1 B.C. It was found many years later in a Danish bog.

THREE MOTHERS

To the Celts, the number three was a sign of power, so they often portrayed their gods and goddesses in triple form. This stone carving shows three mother-goddesses. It was made in Britain, probably between A.D. 50 and A.D. 400. The figures stand for the three female qualities of strength, power, and fertility.

4 Cover both sides of the cardboard strip and the clay figures with glue. Then cover with silver foil. Make sure that the foil is well glued to the figures.

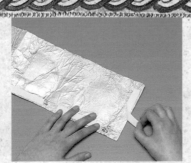

5 Stick double-sided tape to the back of the foil-covered strip along the bottom and side edges. This will be used to join the sides of the bowl.

6 Make holes with an awl every inch or so through the bottom of the strip. Make matching holes along the top of the bowl, as shown.

7 Attach the strip to the bowl with the double-sided tape. Stick the ends together, as shown. Secure by putting paper fasteners through both sets of holes.

Annual Celtic Festivals

A<small>S FARMERS</small>, the Celts needed to be able to measure time, so that they would know when to plough their fields and sow their crops. The Celtic year (354 days) was divided into 12 months, each 29 or 30 days long. Every two-and-a-half years, an extra month was added, so that the calendar kept pace with the natural seasons. The Celts marked the passing of time by holding religious festivals. Samain (November 1) was the most important. It was the beginning of the Celtic year, and was a time for sacrifices and community gatherings. It was a dangerous time, when spirits walked the earth. Samain has survived today in Christian form as All Souls' Day, and Halloween. Imbolc (February 1) marked the beginning of springtime and fertility. Beltane (May 1) was observed by lighting bonfires. Their smoke had purifying powers, and was used to kill pests on cattle. The final festival of the year was Lugnasad (August 1).

GODDESS AND SAINT
This statue is of the Celtic goddess Brigit (later known as St. Brigit in Ireland) who was honored at the Imbolc festival. The Celts believed that she brought fertility and fresh growth. She was also the goddess of learning, and had healing powers.

HOLY DAYS
Celtic calendars were kept by druids (priests). They believed that some days were fortunate, while others brought bad luck. This picture, painted about 150 years ago, shows how one artist thought a druid might look. However, it is mostly imaginary.

MAKE A PIG
You will need: modeling clay, board, modeling tool, ruler, 4 x balsa-wood sticks, metallic paint, paintbrush.

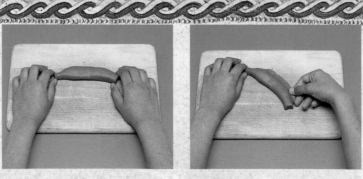

1 Make the body of the pig by rolling a piece of modeling clay into a sausage shape roughly 5 x 5¼ in. Make a head shape at one end.

2 With your thumb and index finger, carefully flatten out a ridge along the back of the pig. The ridge should be about ½ in. high.

3 Now use the modeling tool to make a pattern along the ridge section. The pattern should have straight vertical lines on both sides of the ridge.

CLEVER GOD

Archaeologists think that this stone head, found in North Wales, may represent Lug, the Celtic god of all the arts. According to legend, Lug was clever at everything. He was honored at Lugnasad, the fourth and final festival of the Celtic year when offerings were made to all the earth spirits and goddesses, to ask them for a plentiful harvest.

MISTLETOE AND OAK

Both mistletoe and oak were sacred to the Celts. Druids made sacrifices at wooden temples or in sacred oak groves. Even the druids' name meant "knowledge of the oak." Mistletoe was magic and mysterious. It could only be cut with a golden sickle. Mistletoe growing on oak trees was the most holy and powerful of all.

mistletoe

oak tree leaves

DRUID CEREMONY

This picture from the 1800s shows an imaginary view of druids at a Celtic religious ceremony. We have very little detailed information about how these ceremonies were performed. According to Roman writers, there were three different kinds of druids, each with different duties. Some were soothsayers, who told the future and issued warnings. Some held sacrifices. Some wrote and performed songs in honor of the gods.

To the Celts, wild boars were magic symbols of strength, fertility, and power. The Celts also enjoyed roast boar at feasts held to celebrate the great festivals of the Celtic year, such as Samain, Imbolc, Beltane and Lugnasad.

4 Roll out four legs roughly 2 in. long. Push a balsa-wood stick into each leg. Leave about ½ in. of balsa wood exposed, as shown.

5 Now roll out a small amount of modeling clay. Cut out two triangular shapes using your modeling tool. These will be the pig's ears.

6 Carefully attach the ears on either side of the pig's head. Attach them using a little water and your modeling tool, as shown.

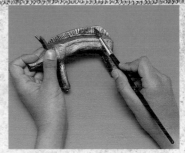

7 Attach the legs to the pig, pushing the balsa wood sticks into the body. Let the modeling clay dry. When it is dry, paint the whole pig.

Gods of the Vikings

WORSHIPPING FREYA

This silver charm shows Freya. She was the goddess of love and marriage, and was particularly popular in Sweden. Freya was the sister of Frey, the god of farming. It was also believed that when women died, Freya would welcome them into the next world. In *Egil's Saga*, a dying woman says "I have not eaten and shall not till I am with Freya."

T HE VIKINGS believed that the universe was held up by a great ash tree called Yggdrasil. The universe was made up of several separate worlds. Niflheim was the underworld, a misty realm of snow and ice. The upper world was Asgard, home of the gods. Its great hall was called Valholl (Valhalla), and it was here that warriors who died bravely in battle came to feast. The world of humans was called Midgard. It was surrounded by a sea of monsters and linked to Asgard by a rainbow bridge. Beyond the sea lay Utgard, the forest home of the Giants, deadly enemies of the gods.

The Vikings believed in many gods. They thought that Odin, father of the gods, rode through the night sky. Odin's wife was Frigg (a day of the week—Friday—is named after her) and his son was Baldr, god of the summer Sun. Powerful, red-bearded Thor was the god of thunder. Like many of the Vikings themselves, he enjoyed laughing, but was quick to anger. The twins Frey and Freya were god and goddess of fertility and love. Trouble was stirred up by Loki, a mischief-making god.

THOR'S HAMMER

This lucky charm from Iceland shows Thor. He used his magic hammer to fight the giants. Thor was strong and brave.

BALDR IS SLAIN

Stories tell how the wicked Loki told the blind god Hod to aim a mistletoe spear at Baldr, god of the Sun and light.

MAKE A LUCKY CHARM

You will need: thick paper or cardboard, pencil, scissors, self-drying clay, board, felt-tip pen, modeling tool, rolling pin, fine sandpaper, silver acrylic paint, brush, water pot, a length of cord.

1 Draw the outline of Thor's hammer onto thick paper or cardboard and cut it out. Use this as the pattern for making your lucky charm, or

2 Place a lump of the clay on the board and roll it flat. Press your cardboard pattern into the clay so that it leaves an outline of the hammer.

3 Remove the card. Use a modeling tool to cut into the clay. Follow around the edge of the imprint as shown, and peel away the hammer shape.

ODIN

One-eyed Odin was the wisest god. He had two ravens called Hugin, meaning thought, and Mugin, meaning memory. Each day the ravens flew across the world. Every evening they flew back to Odin to perch on his shoulders and report to him the deeds that they had seen.

SLEIPNIR

Odin rode across the sky on Sleipnir, a gray, eight-legged horse. A pair of wolves traveled with Odin. In this carved stone from Sweden, Odin and Sleipnir are arriving at Valholl. They would have been welcomed by a *valkyrie*, or servant of the gods, bearing wine for Odin to drink.

Vikings wore lucky charms or amulets to protect themselves from evil. Many of the charms, such as this hammer, honored the god Thor.

4 Model a flattened end to the hammer, as shown. Use a modeling tool to make a hole at the end, to thread the cord through when it is dry.

5 Use the end of a felt-tip pen, a pencil, or modeling tool to press a series of patterns into the clay, as shown. Let the clay dry and harden.

6 When the amulet is dry, smooth any rough edges with sandpaper. Paint one side silver. Let it dry before painting the other side.

7 When the paint has dried, take enough cord to fit your neck and thread it through the hole in the hammer. Cut it with the scissors and tie a knot.

Vikings Convert to Christianity

BY THE BEGINNING of the Viking Age, most of western Europe had become Christian. The early Vikings despised the Christian monks for being meek and mild. The warriors looted church treasures on their raids and murdered many priests or sold them into slavery. However, over the years, some Vikings found it convenient to become Christian. This made it easier for them to trade with merchants in western Europe and to hire themselves out as soldiers with Christian armies.

Christian missionaries went to Scandinavia from Germany and the British Isles. Monks from Constantinople preached to the Vikings living in the Ukraine and Russia. They soon gained followers. In about A.D. 960, King Harald Bluetooth of Denmark became a Christian. In A.D. 995, Olaf Tryggvason, a Christian king, came to the throne of Norway. He pulled down many of the shrines to the old gods. In 1000 the Viking colonists on Iceland also voted to become Christian. The new faith spread from there to Greenland. Sweden was the last Viking country to become Christian. People gave up worshipping pagan gods in the old temples of the settlement at Uppsala.

NEW FAITH
This silver crucifix was found in the Gotland region of Sweden. It is nearly 1,000 years old. It shows Christ wearing short pants, like those worn by Viking men.

STAVE CHURCH
This Christian church is made of staves, or split tree trunks. It was built in Gol, in Norway, in about 1200. The very first Christian churches in Scandinavia were built in this way. When the wooden foundations rotted away, the churches were rebuilt.

SIGN OF THE CROSS
This stone was raised at Jelling in Denmark by King Harald Bluetooth, in honor of his parents. It dates from about A.D. 985. The stone marks a turning point in Viking history—the conversion of the Danes to Christianity. One side of the stone shows a dragon-like beast fighting with a snake. The other side is a Christian scene (*above*), showing Jesus on the cross.

CHOICE OF GODS

The mold below was made from a soft mineral called soapstone. It was used to shape metal pendants 1,000 years ago. The mold could produce both hammer-of-Thor designs and crosses (*above*). The two religions —the old and the new—existed side-by-side for many years in the Viking world. It was a long time before Christianity really took hold. Many of the early converts to Christianity still turned to Thor for help in the heat of battle.

crucifix

Thor's hammer charms

mould

BAPTISM IN A BARREL

The Danish king, Harald Bluetooth, was converted to Christianity in about A.D. 960. This gold altarpiece shows Harald being baptized in a barrel of holy water by Bishop Poppo. Harald went on to build a Christian church on the ancient site of the royal burial mound at Jelling.

AGAINST EVIL

Is this a silver cross, or a hammer-of-Thor charm with a dragon's head? Perhaps it was both. It was certainly intended to protect the wearer from evil and bad luck. Even after they became Christians, the Vikings remained very superstitious people. Helgi the Lean is described in a Viking saga as believing in Christ "yet he still asked Thor for help on sea voyages and when facing danger."

STONE CROSS

This cross is from Kirkinner Church, in Scotland. It is about 1,000 years old. Its carving shows a mixture of Anglian and Norwegian Viking styles. The Christians in Britain, France and Germany were horrified by the Vikings' pagan religion, and they tried to persuade them to give it up. Eventually, Viking kings saw that becoming Christian could make them more powerful.

Spirits in North America

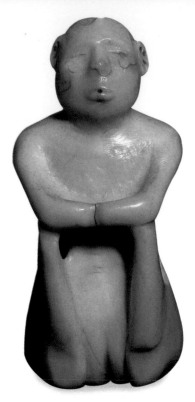

To North American Indian tribes, everything in the world had a soul or spirit that was very powerful and could help or harm humans. They believed that the changing seasons and events surrounding them were caused by different spirits. Spirits had to be treated with respect, so prayers, songs, chants, and dances would be offered to please them. The most important spirit to Sioux tribes was Wakan Tanka, the Great Spirit or Great Mysterious, who was in charge of all other spirits. The Navajo tribes believed in the Holy People. These were Sky, Earth, Moon, Sun, Hero Twins, Thunders, Winds, and Changing Woman. Some tribes believed in ghosts. Western Shoshonis, Salish (Flathead) people, and Ojibwas considered ghosts to be spirit helpers who acted as bodyguards in battle. The leader of ceremonies was the shaman (medicine man) who conducted the dances and rites. He also acted as a doctor. The shamans of California would treat a sick person by sucking out the pain, spitting it out, and sending it away.

CHARMED LIFE
A whale's tusk was used to carve this Inuit shaman's charm. Spirits called tuneraks were thought to help the angakok, as the Inuit shaman was called, in his duties. The role of shaman was passed from father to son. In Padlimuit, Copper, and Iglulik tribes, women could also be shamans.

BEAR NECESSITIES OF LIFE
This shaman is nicknamed Bear's Belly and belonged to the Arikara Plains tribe. Shamans were powerful, providing the link between humans and spirits. After years of training, they could cure ill health, tell the future, or speak to the dead.

MAKE A RATTLE
You will need: thick cardboard, pencil, ruler, scissors, masking tape, compasses, white glue, brush, two balsa wood strips 1 in. wide and 7 in. long, raffia or string, air-drying clay, wooden skewer stick, cream, black, orange/red and brown paint, paintbrushes, water pot, black thread, needle.

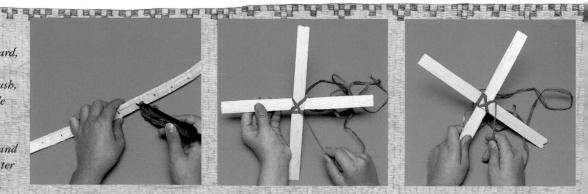

1 Cut two pieces of cardboard ½ in. wide, one 18 in. long and one 22¾ in. long. Cover both in masking tape. Make holes about 1¼ in. apart along the strips.

2 Bend each strip into a ring. Glue and tape the ends together to make two rings. Fix the two strips of balsa wood into a cross to fit across the large ring.

3 Glue the two sticks together, then strap them with raffia or string. Wrap the string around one side then cross it over the center. Repeat on all sides.

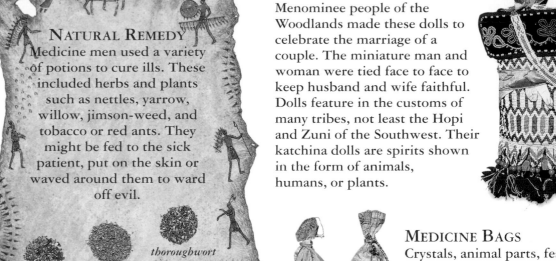

NATURAL REMEDY

Medicine men used a variety of potions to cure ills. These included herbs and plants such as nettles, yarrow, willow, jimson-weed, and tobacco or red ants. They might be fed to the sick patient, put on the skin or waved around them to ward off evil.

thoroughwort

yarrow

skunk cabbage

willow bark

THE HAPPY COUPLE

Menominee people of the Woodlands made these dolls to celebrate the marriage of a couple. The miniature man and woman were tied face to face to keep husband and wife faithful. Dolls feature in the customs of many tribes, not least the Hopi and Zuni of the Southwest. Their katchina dolls are spirits shown in the form of animals, humans, or plants.

MEDICINE BAGS

Crystals, animal parts, feathers and powders made of ground up plants and vegetables might be inside these bundles. They were used to make cures and spells by a shaman (medicine man) of the Winnebago tribe from the Woodlands.

SACRED BIRD

Rattles such as this Thunderbird rattle from the Northwest Coast were considered sacred objects and carved with the images of spirits. They were made of animal hoofs, rawhide, or turtle shells, and filled with seeds or pebbles. Some were hand-held, others were put on necklaces.

Rattles were an important part of any ceremony. In some tribes only shamans could hold one.

4 Glue the two cardboard rings onto the cross, as here. The larger ring sits on the outer ends of the cross. The smaller one is roughly ¼ in. inside of that.

5 Roll out the modeling clay to a ½ in. thickness. Cut out 20 to 30 semicircle shapes to resemble penguin beaks. Use a stick to make a hole at one end.

6 When the beaks are dry, paint them cream. Let dry. Paint the tips black then paint red or orange stripes. Next, paint the two rings brown.

7 Thread the black cotton through the hole in a painted beak, then tie it through one of the holes in the rings. Repeat with each beak, filling both rings.

American Indian Purifying Rites

STEAM AND SMOKE
A holy man, such as this Pima shaman, would be in charge of sweats. Prayers and chants were offered and the sacred pipe was passed around each time the door was opened.

SWEATING PURIFIED THE BODY AND MIND according to North American Indians. The Sioux called it "fire without end." The sweat was one of the most important and ancient of all North American religious rituals. They were among the first people to use heat to cleanse the body. But for tribe members, it was not simply a question of hygiene. The sweat lodge rite was performed before and after other ceremonies to symbolize moving into and out of a sacred world. Warriors prepared their spirits before the Sun Dance ceremony by taking a sweat bath. This was a dance to give thanks for food and gifts received during the year, and often featured self-mutilation. Sweats were also taken as a medical treatment to cure illness, and as a rite of passage through a stage in life such as from childhood to adulthood. A young boy who was about to make his transition into warrior-life was invited to spend time with the tribe's males. They would offer him the sacred pipe, which was usually smoked to send prayers. This was called Hunka's ceremony and showed the tribe's acceptance that the boy was ready. Some warrior initiation rites were brutal—such as the Mandan's custom of suspending young men by wooden hooks pierced through their chest, or scarring them, known as Okipa. Both girls and boys prepared for passing into adolescence by spending time alone and fasting (not eating).

BUILDING A SWEAT LODGE
These two Indian girls stand beside their family sweat lodge. Two main types of lodges were used, the earth-covered lodge or this variety, built of saplings then covered with blankets, canvas, or hide. The blankets would be removed between sweats. The stones were heated outside then carried in. Steam was created by pouring water over the stones.

BATHS IN EARTH

An Indian crawls out from an earth-covered sweat lodge for air. Six to eight people could sit around the hot stones inside, depending on the size of the sweat lodge. Males and females would both take part in sweats but it was customary to do so separately. In some tribes, families built their own family lodges and some larger sweat lodges were also used as homes or temples. Sticks and wood formed the frame. This was covered in mud or clay. The fire would be built in the lodge causing a dry heat. It was dark, stuffy, and hot, similar to the saunas used in Europe. However, a sweat lodge was used to cleanse the spirit as well as the skin.

CLEANSED AND REFRESHED

Herbs, such as sweetgrass and cedar, were often put on the hot stones inside a sweat lodge. When the water was poured over the stones, the smell and essence of the herbs were released into the lodge with the steam. Herbs helped to clear the nasal passages. They could also be selected to treat particular ills. As the heat from the steam opened up the skin's pores, the herbs could enter the body and work at the illness or help purify the spirit. Sweating removed toxins (poisons in the body) and, the Indians believed, forced out disease.

GROWING UP

A young Apache girl is dressed up for a modern tribal ceremony. The lives of North American Indians were filled with rituals to mark each milestone in a person's life or important tribal events. There were ceremonies for birth, for becoming an adult, or to mark changing seasons.

INSTRUMENTS TELL A STORY

This Tsimshian rattle has been involved in many ceremonies. Tribes had a vast amount of ceremonial objects, from rattles to headdresses, clothing, and wands. Their decorations were usually of spiritual significance. In some tribes, the frog was respected since it would croak when danger was near. Others believed that their long tongues could suck out evil. A frog also features in the creation myths of the Nez Perce.

Shamans in the Arctic World

Long before Christian missionaries arrived in the Arctic, local people had developed their own beliefs. Arctic people thought that all living creatures possessed a spirit or *inua*. When an animal died, its spirit lived on and was reborn in another creature. Powerful spirits were thought to control the natural world, and these invisible forces influenced people's everyday lives. Some spirits were believed to be friendly towards humans. Others were malevolent or harmful. People showed their respect for the spirits by obeying taboos—rules that surrounded every aspect of life. If a taboo was broken the spirit would be angered. People called shamans could communicate with the spiritual world. Shamans had many different roles in the community. They performed rituals to bring good luck in hunting, predicted the weather, the movements of the reindeer herds, and helped to heal the sick. They worked as doctors, priests, and prophets, all rolled into one.

SHAMAN AND DRUM
An engraving from the early 1800s shows a female shaman from Siberia. Most, but not all, shamans were male. Shamans often sang and beat on special drums, such as the one shown above, to enter a trance. Some drums had symbols drawn on them and helped the shamans to predict the future.

TUPILAK CARVING
This little ivory carving from Greenland shows a monster called a *tupilak. Tupilaks* were evil spirits. If someone wished an enemy harm, he might secretly make a little carving similar to this, which would bring a real *tupilak* to life. It would destroy the enemy unless the person possessed even more powerful magic to ward it off.

SHAMAN'S DRUM

You will need: ruler, scissors, thick cardboard, white glue, glue brush, masking tape, compass, pencil, chamois leather, brown paint, paint brush, water pot, brown thread or string

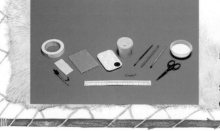

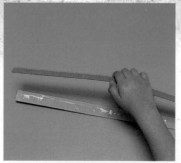

1 Cut out two strips of thick cardboard, each strip measuring 30¼ in. long and 1¼ in. wide. Glue the two strips together to give the cardboard extra thickness.

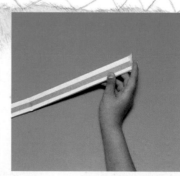

2 Once the glue has dried, use masking tape to cover the edges of the double-thickness cardboard. Try to make the edges as neat as possible.

3 Using a compass, draw a circle with a 9½ in. diameter on a piece of chamois leather. Cut it out, leaving a ¾ in. strip around the edge of the circle.

HERBAL MEDICINES

An Innu woman collects pitcher plants that she will use to make herbal medicines. In ancient times, shamans acted as community doctors. They made medicines from plants and gave them to sick people to heal them. They also entered trances to soothe angry spirits, which helped the sick to recover from their illness.

SEA SPIRIT

This beautiful Inuit sculpture shows a powerful spirit called Sedna. The Inuit believed that Sedna controlled storms and all sea creatures. If anyone offended Sedna, she withheld her blessing and hunting was poor. Here Sedna is portrayed with a mermaid's tail and accompanied by a narwhal and two seals. This very delicate carving has been made from a piece of reindeer antler.

MAGIC MASK

This mask is from Arctic North America. It was worn by Inuit shamans during a special ritual to communicate with the spirit world. Shamans wore wooden masks similar to this one. They also wore headdresses. Each mask represented a powerful spirit. The shaman would call on the spirit by chanting, dancing, and beating on a special drum.

Shamans' drums were made of deerskin stretched over a round wooden frame. The shaman sometimes drew pictures of people, animals, and stars on the side of the drum.

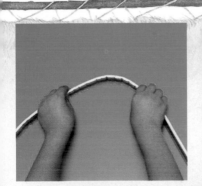

4 Using your fingers, curve the strip of cardboard, as shown above. Make sure you curve the cardboard slowly so that it does not crease.

5 Glue the cardboard onto the circle. Ask someone to help keep the chamois leather stretched as you go. Tape the ends of the cardboard together.

6 Make cuts 1 in. apart along the edge of the excess chamois leather towards the cardboard, as shown above. Glue the edges to the cardboard

7 Paint the cardboard with dark brown paint and let it dry. Decorate the drum with thick brown thread or string by tying it around the edges.

Aztec Myths and Omens

THE AZTECS OF CENTRAL AMERICA lived in constant fear that their world might come to an end. Ancient legends told that this had happened four times before. Each time, the world had been born again. Yet Aztec priests and astrologers did not believe that this would happen next time. If the world ended again, it would be forever. The souls of all Aztec people would be banished to a dark, gloomy underworld. The Wind of Knives would cut the flesh from their bones, and living skeletons would feast and dance with the Lord of the Dead. Then the Aztecs would vanish forever when they reached Mictlan (hell). The Maya people told similar stories about the underworld—which they called Xibalba (the Place of Fright) in a great epic poem, the *Popol Vuh*. This poem featured two brothers, called the Hero Twins.

Aztec legends also told that the end of the world would be heralded by strange signs. In A.D. 1519, these gloomy prophecies seemed to be coming true. Ruler Moctezuma II had weird, worrying dreams. Astronomers also observed eclipses of the Sun and a moving comet with a fiery tail.

FEATHERED SERPENT
Quetzalcoatl was an ancient god-king. His name meant feathered serpent. He was worshipped by many Mesoamerican people, but especially by the Toltecs. They believed that he had sacrificed himself to help his people. A Toltec legend said that one day he would return, heralding the end of the world.

HEROS AND LEGENDS
This ball court is in Copan, Guatemala. The ball game featured in many Maya legends about the Hero Twins. They were skilled ball-game players and also expert hunters with deadly blow guns.

CREATURES OF LEGEND

This Maya bowl is decorated with a picture of a spider-monkey. Many different kinds of monkeys lived in the rainforests of Mesoamerica. Monkey-gods played an important part in Maya myths and legends. Because monkeys were quick and clever, the Maya believed that monkey-gods protected clever people, such as scribes.

THE NEW FIRE CEREMONY

Every 52 years, the Aztecs believed that the world might come to an end. To stop this happening, they held a special ceremony. People put out their fires and stayed indoors. At sunset, priests climbed to the top of a hill and waited for the planet Venus to appear in the sky. At the moment it appeared, a captive was sacrificed to the gods. His heart was ripped out and a fire lit in his chest. The priests then sent messengers all over the Aztec lands, carrying torches to relight the fires. People then believed the world was safe for another 52 years.

HEAVENLY MESSENGER

Ruler Moctezuma is shown here observing the brilliant comet that appeared in the Mexican sky in 1519. Priests and Aztec people carefully studied the stars for messages from the gods. They remembered the old Toltec legend that said one day, the god Quetzalcoatl would return and bring the world to an end.

AZTEC HERITAGE

Many Aztec and Maya traditions still survive today. Millions of people speak Nahuatl (the Aztecs' language) or Maya languages. Aztec and Maya beliefs have mingled with Christian traditions to create new religious festivals. The most famous of these festivals is the Day of the Dead. Families bring presents of flowers and sweets shaped like skulls to their ancestors' graves.

Blood Sacrifices of Mesoamerica

MESOAMERICAN PEOPLE, such as the Aztecs and Maya, believed that unless they made offerings of blood and human lives to the gods, the Sun would die and the world would come to an end. Maya rulers pricked themselves with cactus thorns and sting-ray spines, or drew spiked cords through their tongues to draw blood. They pulled out captives' fingernails so the blood flowed. Aztecs pricked their earlobes each morning and collected two drops of blood to give to the gods. They also went to war to capture prisoners. On special occasions, vast numbers of captives were needed for sacrifice. It was reported that 20,000 victims were sacrificed to celebrate the completion of the Great Temple at Tenochtitlan in 1487. It took four days to kill them all. Mesoamerican temples were tombs as well as places of sacrifice. Rulers and their wives were buried inside. Each ruler aimed to build a great temple as a memorial to his reign.

TEMPLE TOMB
Pyramid Temple 1 at Tikal was built in the A. D. 700s as a memorial to a Maya king. Nine stone platforms were built above the burial chamber, to create a tall pyramid shape reaching up to the sky.

HOLY KNIFE
This sacrificial knife has a blade of a semi-precious stone called chalcedony. It was made by Mixtecs from south Mexico. Mesoamerican priests used finely decorated knives of flint, obsidian, and other hard stones to kill captives for sacrifice. These were trimmed to be as sharp as glass.

A PYRAMID TEMPLE

You will need: pencil, ruler, thick cardboard, scissors, white glue, glue brush, masking tape, thin strips of balsa wood, thin cardboard, corrugated cardboard, water bowl, paintbrushes, paints.

Bottom level A x2 — 17¾ in. — 17¾ in.
Top level C — 8¼ in. — 8¼ in. — A x4 — 17¾ in.
Middle level B x2 — 13 in. — 13 in. — 1¼ in. — B x4 — 13 in. — C x4 — 2 in. — ¾ in. — 28¾ in.
2¼ in. — 2¼ in. — 3½ in. x6 — 3½ in. x2 — Shrine roof — Shrine walls — x 2 — 2¼ in. — 2¼ in. — 2¼ in. — 2¼ in. — 2¼ in.

Cut out pieces for the pyramid and temple-top shrines from thick cardboard, as shown.

1 Use white glue and masking tape to join the thick cardboard pieces to make three flat boxes (A, B, and C). Leave the boxes until the glue is completely

2 From the remaining pieces of cardboard, make the two temple-top shrines, as shown. You could add extra details with strips of balsa wood or thin

SKULL SHRINE

Rows of human skulls, carved in stone, decorate this shrine outside the Aztecs' Great Temple in the center of Tenochtitlan. Most Aztec temples also had skull racks, where rows of real human heads were displayed. They were cut from the bodies of sacrificed captives.

RELIGIOUS GIFTS

Mesoamerican people also made offerings of food and flowers as gifts to the gods. Maize was a valuable gift because it was the Mesoamerican people's most important food. Bright orange marigolds were a sign of the Sun, on which every person's life depended.

maize

marigolds

PERFECTION

The ideal victim for human sacrifice was a fit and healthy young man.

HUMAN SACRIFICE

This Aztec codex painting shows captives being sacrificed. At the top, you can see a priest cutting open a captive's chest and removing the heart as an offering to the gods.

This model is based on the Great Temple that stood in the center of Tenochtitlan.

3 Glue the boxes, one on top of the next. Cut out pieces of cardboard the same size as each side of your boxes. They should be about ¾ in. wide. Stick down, as shown.

4 Cut out two strips of cardboard ¾ x 10¼ in. Glue them to a third piece of cardboard 5½ x 10¼ in. Glue corrugated cardboard 3¾ x 10¼ in. in position.

5 Stick the staircase to the front of the temple, as shown. Use a ruler to check that the staircase is an equal distance from either side of the temple.

6 Paint the whole temple a cream color to look like natural stone. Add details, such as carvings or wall paintings, using brightly colored paint.

Inca Feasts and Celebrations

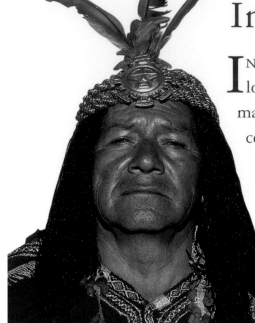

IN COMMON WITH OTHER CENTRAL AMERICAN PEOPLE, the Incas loved to celebrate the natural world and its changing seasons. They marked them with special festivals and religious rituals. Some celebrations were held in villages and fields, others took place at religious sites or in the cities. It is said that the Incas had as many as 150 festivals each year. The biggest festival of all was *Inti Raymi*, the Feast of the Sun. It was held in June, to mark midwinter in the southern part of the world. *Qapaq Raymi*, the Splendid Festival, was held in December to mark the southern midsummer. This was when boys were recognized as adult warriors or young nobles. Crop festivals included the Great Ripening each February, the Earth Ripening each March, and the Great Cultivation each May. The sowing of new maize was celebrated in August. The Feast of the Moon, held in September, was a special festival for women, while the Day of the Dead, in November, was a time to honor one's ancestors.

FEAST OF THE SUN
The Quechua people of Peru have revived the ancient festival of *Inti Raymi*. They gather each year at Sacsahuaman fortress, Cuzco, to celebrate the light and warmth of the Sun during the southern midwinter. In Inca times, a golden bowl was raised to the rising Sun. The Sun's rays would be used to make fire.

BRINGER OF RAIN
Drought was feared throughout the Empire, especially in the dry lands of the coast. If rain failed to fall, the life-giving irrigation channels dried up. In desperation, people visited the temples of Apu Illapu, bringer of rain. The priests made offerings and sacrifices, and the pilgrims prayed. The purpose of most Inca ceremonies and festivals was to prevent disaster and to ensure that life carried on.

THE AUGUST FESTIVAL
Quya Raymi (August) was a rainy month. A special festival called *Situa* was held to ward off the sicknesses that were common at that time of year. The people dressed for battle and went out into the streets. They hoped to drive away the evil spirits that made them ill. They carried torches of burning straw and plastered their faces with cornmeal or llama blood.

DANCERS AND MASKS

Drums, music, and dance were always an important part of *Inti Raymi*, the Sun Festival. The Incas played rattles and whistles, drums and hand drums, flutes and panpipes to help them celebrate the festival. Musicians played all day long without taking a break, and some of their ancient tunes are still known. Today, masks representing the Spanish invaders are added to the festivities. The modern festival proves that the old way of life has not been forgotten. Modern Peruvians are proud of their Inca past.

THE EMPEROR'S DAY

The modern festival of *Inti Raymi* attracts thousands to Cuzco. In the days of the Incas, too, nobles poured into the Inca capital from every corner of the Empire. Their aim was to honor the emperor as much as the Sun god. They came carrying tributes from the regions and personal gifts, hoping for the Emperor's favor in return.

FIESTA TIME

A drawing from the 1700s shows Peruvian dancers dressed as devils. Many of them are playing musical instruments or carrying long whips. After the conquest, festivals were known by the Spanish term, *fiestas*, and officially celebrated Christian beliefs. However, many of the festivities were still rooted in an Inca past. The dances and costumes often had their origins in Inca traditions.

Glossary

A

ancestor A family member who died long ago.

archaeologist Someone who studies ancient ruins and artifacts to learn about the past.

Arctic The region in the far north of our planet, surrounding the North Pole.

Aztecs Mesoamerican people who lived in northern and central Mexico. They were at their most powerful between A.D. 1350 and A.D. 1520.

B

bard In Celtic times, bards were well-educated poets. Becoming a bard was the first stage in the long training of a druid (a Celtic priest).

Buddha A Indian prince who left his family to seek enlightenment. Founder of the Buddhist way of life.

C

chalcedony A reddish semi-precious stone.

chullpa A burial chamber in the form of a tower.

codex A folding book used by the Aztec people of Central America.

D

Daoism Chinese philosophy based on contemplation of the natural world. It later became a religion with a belief in magic.

deity A god or goddess.

druid Celtic priests. According to Roman writers, there were three different grades of druids. Some studied the natural world and claimed to foretell the future. Some were bards who knew about history. Some led Celtic worship, made sacrifices to the gods, and administered holy laws.

dynasty A period of rule by the same royal family.

E

embalm To preserve a dead body.

empire An area including many cities and countries, and ruled by one person.

F

festival A special day set aside to honor a god or goddess.

H

human sacrifice Killing humans as an offering to a god.

hunter-gatherer A person whose way of life involves hunting wild animals and gathering plant foods.

I

immortal An idea or person that can live forever.

inua An Inuit word for spirit.

Inuit The native people of the Arctic regions of North America, Canada, and Greenland as distinguished from Asia and the Aleutian Islands. Inuit is also the name for an Eskimo in Canada.

irrigation Bringing water to dry lands so that crops can grow.

ivory The hard, smooth, cream-colored part of the tusks of elephants or walruses.

K

kami Japanese holy spirits.

L

llama A camel-like creature of South America. It is shorn for its wool and was sacrificed in ceremonies by the Inca people.

M

Maya People who lived in southwestern Mexico, Guatamala, and Belize. The

Maya lands were conquered by the Spanish between A.D. 1524 and A.D. 1546.

mummification The process of preserving a human or animal body, by drying.

mummy A dead body preserved by being dried out in the sun, by extreme cold, or by a mixture of chemicals.

myth An ancient story about gods and heroes.

N

Neanderthals A group of *homo sapiens* who were the first people to bury their dead.

P

Panathenaic festival A yearly procession with sacrifices in honor of Athena, that took place at the Parthenon in Athens.

Parthenon A temple in Greece on the Acropolis in Athens dedicated to the city's goddess, Athena.

pharaoh Title given to the the most powerful ruler in ancient Egypt.

pilgrim A person who makes a journey to a holy place.

prehistoric Belonging to the time before written records were made.

propylaea The monumental gateways to the temple complex on top of the Acropolis in Athens in Greece.

pyramid A large pointed monument with a square base and triangular sides.

R

rites Solemn procedures carried out for a religious purpose or ceremony.

rituals An often repeated set of actions carried out during a religious ceremony.

S

sacrifice The killing of a living thing in honor of the gods.

sanctuary The most holy place in a temple.

shamans Medicine men or women in tribal cultures. These people were healers, doctors, spiritual, and ceremonial leaders.

Shinto An ancient Japanese religion, known as "the way of the gods" based on honoring holy spirits.

shrine A container of holy relics or a place for worship.

sultan A Muslim ruler.

symbol A mark that has a special meaning.

T

taboo A rule or custom linked with a religious belief that shows respect to the spirit.

temple A special building where a god or goddess is worshipped.

Torii The traditional gateway to a Shinto shrine.

tribe A group of families who owe loyalty to a chief.

turban Headdress worn by Muslim, Sikh and some Hindu men.

U

Underworld This was the place to which the spirits of the dead were supposed to travel in ancient Greece.

V

Vaishnavism Hindu belief in Vishnu as lord of the Universe.

Viking One of the Scandinavian peoples who lived by sea-raiding in the Middle Ages.

Venus figurine A statue of a woman, usually shown with large hips, breasts and buttocks, and a full stomach. The figurines may have been worshipped as symbols of fertility or plenty, or carried as good luck charms.

Index